50 I  a

Waterfall on the Baptism River, Tettegouche State Park

50 *Hikes*
in Minnesota

Day Hikes from Forest to Prairie to River Bluff

GWEN RUFF & BEN WOIT

The Countryman Press
Woodstock, Vermont

An Invitation to the Reader

Over time trails can be rerouted and signs and landmarks altered. If you find that changes have occurred on the routes described in this book, please let us know so that corrections may be made in future editions. The author and publisher also welcome other comments and suggestions. Address all correspondence to:

Editor, *50 Hikes*™ Series
The Countryman Press
P.O. Box 748
Woodstock, VT 05091

Library of Congress
Cataloging-in-Publication Data
has been applied for.
ISBN 0-88150-622-2

Maps by Mapping Specialists Ltd.,
  © The Countryman Press
Book design by Glenn Suokko
Text composition by Chelsea Cloeter
Cover photograph by G. Alan Nelson
Interior photographs by the authors

Copyright © 2005 by Gwen Ruff

First edition

Published by The Countryman Press
P.O. Box 748
Woodstock, VT 05091

Distributed by W. W. Norton & Company Inc.
500 Fifth Avenue
New York, NY 10110

Printed in the United States of America

10 9 8 7 6 5 4 3 2 1

ACKNOWLEDGMENTS

Many of these hikes were done with family. Thanks to daughter Claire, son Andy, brother Doug, brother-in-law Randy, nieces Anna and Abby, and nephew Ezra for sharing the trails with us. Doug and Randy also wielded cameras, and we appreciate their help.

Thanks also to the employees at Minnesota's state and national parks and forests. These people seem to love their jobs, and it shows in their helpfulness, courtesy, and knowledge. They are a human resource that makes spending time among the state's natural resources that much better.

Finally, Gwen would like to thank Ben for collaborating on this project. It's been great sharing time before he starts his own hike through life.

50 Hikes in Minnesota at a Glance

HIKE	REGION	DISTANCE (miles)	DIFFICULTY	GOOD FOR KIDS
1. Banning State Park	Coniferous	3	E/M	★
2. Bear Head Lake State Park	Coniferous	4.2	M	★
3. Cascade River State Park	Coniferous	7.8	M-D	
4. Chippewa National Forest, Shingobee Recreation Area, and North Country Trail	Coniferous	3	E-M	★
5. George H. Crosby–Manitou State Park	Coniferous	2.6	M-D	
6. Gooseberry Falls State Park	Coniferous	2.5	M-D	
7. Grand Portage State Park	Coniferous	2.7	M	★
8. Itasca State Park	Coniferous	4.2	E	★
9. Jay Cooke State Park	Coniferous	4	M	★
10. Judge C. R. Magney State Park	Coniferous	2.5	M-D, lots of steps	★
11. Lake Walk, Superior Hiking Trail	Coniferous	1.6	E	★
12. Mille Lacs Kathio State Park	Coniferous	3.2	M-D	★
13. Oberg Mountain	Coniferous	2.4	M	★EC
14. Savanna Portage State Park	Coniferous	5.4	E	★
15. Split Rock River, Superior Hiking Trail	Coniferous	5	M+	★EC
16. Split Rock Lighthouse State Park	Coniferous	2	M+	★
17. St. Croix State Forest	Coniferous	9.5	M	Length may be a factor
18. St. Croix State Park	Coniferous	6.5	E	★

Legend

DIFFICULTY RATINGS:
E   Easy
M   Moderate
D   Difficult

FEATURES:
G   geology
H   history
L   lake

R   river
SV scenic view
UH unusual habitat
WF waterfall

FEATURE	PLACES TO STAY	OTHER ACTIVITIES	NOTES
G, H, R, SV	C, OL	C, S, W	Historic quarry remains, river rapids
L	C, OL	C, S, W	
G, R, SV, WF	C	C, S,W-EC	Numerous river cascades
L	C	C, S, W	
G, R, SV, WF	C	S, W	Primitive wilderness park
G, R, SV, WF	C	C, S, W	Well-known waterfall
G, H, R, SV, WF		S, W	Historic voyageur area, nearby national historic site
H, L, R, SV	C, OL	C, S	Headwaters of the Mississippi River
G, R, SV	C, OL	C, S, W	Unique geology
G, R, SV, WF	C	C, S	Unique waterfall
G, L, SV		S, W	Lake Superior shoreline
H, L	C, OL	C, S	Ancient Native American sites
SV		S, W-EC	Many scenic vistas
G, H, L, SV, UH	C, OL	C, S	Bog walk, historic portage trail
G, R, SV	C	S, W in some sections	Interesting geology
G, H, L, SV	C	C, S	Historic lighthouse
L, R, SV	C		
R, SV	C, OL	C, S, W	

GOOD FOR KIDS:
EC   exercise caution

PLACES TO STAY:
C   camping
C*   campsites accessible by water only
OL   other lodging

OTHER ACTIVITIES:
C   cross-country skiing
S   snowshoeing
W   winter hiking
EC   Exercise caution

50 Hikes in Minnesota at a Glance

HIKE	REGION	DISTANCE (miles)	DIFFICULTY	GOOD FOR KIDS
19. Sturgeon River Trail	Coniferous	2.5	E	★
20. Superior National Forest, Bass Lake Trail	Coniferous	5.6	M	★EC
21. Superior National Forest, George Washington Memorial Pines Trail	Coniferous	2.3	E	★
22. Superior National Forest and Boundary Waters Canoe Area Wilderness, Eagle Mountain Trail	Coniferous	7	M-D	★EC
23. Superior National Forest and Boundary Waters Canoe Area Wilderness, North Arm Trails	Coniferous	6.1	E	★
24. Temperance River State Park	Coniferous	2.5	E	★EC
25. Tettegouche State Park	Coniferous	11.6	M-D	Length may be a factor
26. Vermilion Gorge Trail	Coniferous	3	M	★EC
27. Voyageurs National Park	Coniferous	3.6	E-M	★
28. Afton State Park	Deciduous	6.5	M	★
29. Forestville/Mystery Cave State Park	Deciduous	7.6	E	★
30. Interstate State Park	Deciduous	3.5	M	★EC
31. Lake Maria State Park	Deciduous	4.5	E	★
32. Minnesota Valley National Wildlife Refuge, Louisville Swamp Unit	Deciduous	9.3	E	Length may be a factor
33. Nerstrand Big Woods State Park	Deciduous	3.2	E	★
34. Sibley State Park	Deciduous	5	M	★

Legend

DIFFICULTY RATINGS:
E   Easy
M   Moderate
D   Difficult

FEATURES:
G   geology
H   history
L   lake

R   river
SV   scenic view
UH   unusual habitat
WF   waterfall

FEATURE	PLACES TO STAY	OTHER ACTIVITIES	NOTES
R, SV	C	C	
G, L, SV, WF	C	W-EC	Interesting geology
H		C	
G, SV	C	W-EC	Highest point in Minnesota, self-issued Boundary Waters permit required for day hiking, regular permit required for overnight within Boundary Waters
G, L, SV	C	C, S, W off groomed trails	Self-issued Boundary Waters permit required
G, R, SV	C	C, S, W-EC	Interesting geology
G, H, L, R, SV, WF	C, OL	C, S	Many scenic vistas, historic cabins
G, H, R, SV, WF		W-EC	Interesting geology
H, L, SV	C*	S	Historic voyageurs area
R, SV	C	C, S, W	
G, H, R, SV	C	C, S, W	Historic site, cave tours
G, R, SV	C	W	Unique geology
L	C, OL	C, S, W	Big Woods remnant
H, R	C	C, S, W	Historic farmstead remains
R, UH	C	C, S	Big Woods remnant, rare plants
L, SV	C	C, S	Highest point within 50 miles

GOOD FOR KIDS:
EC   exercise caution

PLACES TO STAY:
C   camping
C*   campsites accessible by water only
OL   other lodging

OTHER ACTIVITIES:
C   cross-country skiing
S   snowshoeing
W   winter hiking
EC   Exercise caution

50 Hikes in Minnesota at a Glance

HIKE	REGION	DISTANCE (miles)	DIFFICULTY	GOOD FOR KIDS
35. Whitewater State Park	Deciduous	4.2	M-D	★EC
36. Blue Mounds State Park	Prairie Grasslands	4.1	E-M	★EC
37. Buffalo River State Park	Prairie Grasslands	3.3	E	★
38. Fort Ridgely State Park	Prairie Grasslands	3.9	M	★
39. Glacial Lakes State Park	Prairie Grasslands	4.1	M	★
40. Kilen Woods State Park	Prairie Grasslands	2	E	★
41. Lac qui Parle State Park	Prairie Grasslands	3.2	E	★
42. Lower Sioux Agency Historic Site	Prairie Grasslands	2	E-M	★
43. Split Rock Creek State Park	Prairie Grasslands	2.7	E	★
44. Upper Sioux Agency State Park	Prairie Grasslands	2.5	M	★
45. Crow Wing State Park	Mississippi River Banks and Bluffs	4.9	E	★
46. Fort Snelling State Park	Mississippi River Banks and Bluffs	3.6	E	★
47. Frontenac State Park	Mississippi River Banks and Bluffs	3	M-D	★EC
48. Great River Bluffs State Park	Mississippi River Banks and Bluffs	5.7	E-M	★EC
49. Richard J. Dorer Memorial Hardwood State Forest, Trout Valley Unit	Mississippi River Banks and Bluffs	7	M-D	Length may be a factor
50. Spring Lake Park Reserve	Mississippi River	3	E	★EC

Legend

DIFFICULTY RATINGS:
E   Easy
M   Moderate
D   Difficult

FEATURES:
G   geology
H   history
L   lake

R   river
SV   scenic view
UH   unusual habitat
WF   waterfall

FEATURE	PLACES TO STAY	OTHER ACTIVITIES	NOTES
R, SV	C, OL	C, S, W	
G, SV	C	S, W	Unique geology, nearby national historic site
R, SV	C	C, S	Prairie remnant
H, R, SV	C	C, S, W	Historic fort remains
G, L, SV	C, OL	C, S, W	Good examples of glacial landforms
R, SV, UH	C	C, S	Rare plants and calcareous fen, nearby ancient petroglyphs
H, R	C	C, S	Recreated historic mission
H, R			Historic site
L	C	C, S	Historic stone bridge
H, R	C, OL	C, S	Historic site
G, H, R	C, OL	C, S	Historic site
G, H, R		C, S, W	Recreated historic fort with costumed interpreters
G, R, SV	C	C, S, W	Interesting geology
G, R, SV, UH	C	C, S, W	Unique habitat
G, R, SV	C	S, W	Wide variety of wildflowers
G, R, SV		C, S	Banks and Bluffs

GOOD FOR KIDS:
EC   exercise caution

PLACES TO STAY:
C   camping
C*   campsites accessible by water only
OL   other lodging

OTHER ACTIVITIES:
C   cross-country skiing
S   snowshoeing
W   winter hiking
EC   Exercise caution

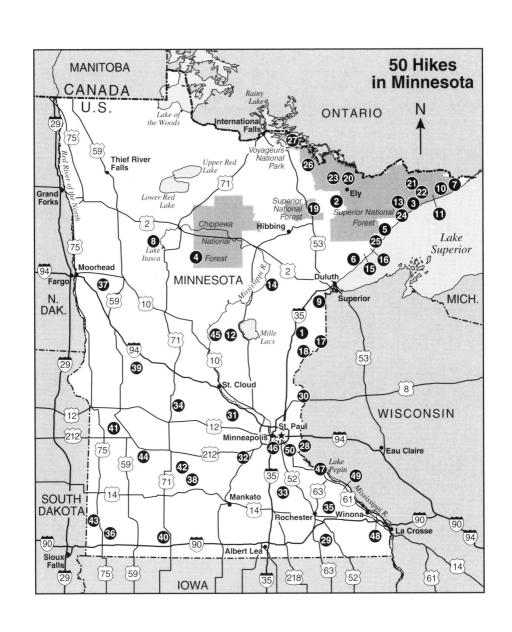

50 Hikes
in Minnesota

CONTENTS

Prairie Grasslands

Mississippi River Banks and Bluffs

Introduction

Minnesotans are known to be extremely partisan about their state. We've got the largest freshwater lake in the world and the start of the country's longest river. We've got pine forests, the deciduous Big Woods, and prairies. We've got rivers and lakes galore. The winters could be shorter, the mosquitoes could be fewer, but you can't have everything. In total, it all adds up to a state of diverse scenic beauty and recreational activities.

Minnesota's Geology

Geology explains why a landscape looks as it does. It influences what plants grow on the land, and which animals feed on and live among those plants. Geology and vegetation affect where people—from native inhabitants to modern settlers—live, and how they make a living.

Minnesota sits on the southern edge of the Canadian Shield, the nucleus of North America that formed during the Precambrian period. Geologists measure this period from when the earth was formed to about 5.7 billion years ago. What is now Minnesota started as barren, uneven bulges in the earth's ancient granite foundation. Some of this oldest known rock is still exposed. In other places, this ancient bedrock is buried under hundreds of feet of younger rock and soil.

Volcanoes of the very early Precambrian period, about 4.5 to 2.5 billion years ago, left rock that alternated with sedimentary belts. Later, the earth bulged and thrust up a mountain range reaching from southwestern Minnesota northeast into Canada. In mid-Precambrian times, about 2.5 to 1.6 billion years ago, Minnesota's iron ranges formed.

Through the millions of years that followed, erosion wore down the mountains, exposing knobs of hard granite and gneiss.

About 1.2 billion years ago, North America began to split apart. Volcanoes broke through cracks to cover much of northeast Minnesota, west to the Mesabi Range, and south to Taylors Falls. Their remains are Minnesota's beloved North Shore of Lake Superior. The tremendous movement that folded the earth's surface and made the dip that became the Great Lake's bed followed shortly.

Vast seas also invaded Minnesota several times. Their sediments formed the Mesabi iron formations and probably quartzite, with its now famous pipestone or catlinite. In the southern part of the state, the sediments formed the sandstone, limestone, and shale in river ledges from Taylors Falls to Iowa. The receding sea left the sediment exposed to erosion, returned again, and once more receded. While land animals developed and smaller, more highly developed life displaced reptiles, the sea made a final thrust toward Minnesota. Thwarted by the Rocky Mountains, this brief resurgence marked the end of the state's marine history.

The effects of older glaciers mostly have been obscured, and the glacial activity that gives Minnesota's landscape its familiar characteristics occurred only about 75,000 to 10,000 years ago. Ice came out of Canada to cover much of the continent, and all of Minnesota except its small southeastern corner. Minnesota owes its fertile soil, undulating surface, and thousands of shallow, water-filled depressions to these glaciers. During those thousands of years, ice lobes made several incursions and retreats. After scouring rock ridges, polishing knolls, breaking off and shoving boulders around, and unloading countless tons of drift, they finally melted, leaving heaped-up debris in the form of innumerable moraines, kettles, and eskers. Debris dammed meltwater to create some of Minnesota's 15,000 lakes. In other cases, huge chunks of ice melted, or water filled glacially gouged depressions.

The retreating ice left huge Lake Agassiz, named in 1879 to honor Louis Agassiz (1807–1873), a young Swiss naturalist who came to teach at Harvard in 1846. He first proposed the theory that glaciers formed the landscape we see now. This body of water, larger than the combined Great Lakes, occupied northwestern Minnesota and extended well into the Dakotas and Canada. It drained southeast through the huge Glacial River Warren, named after General G.K. Warren. The name first appeared in a paper presented before the American Association for the Advancement of Science at an 1883 meeting in Minneapolis. The Minnesota River is a remnant of ancient River Warren. Lake Superior is left over from the much larger and higher Lake Duluth. Barred by the melting glacier from draining through the present Great Lakes channel, Lake Duluth forced an outlet southward and sent its waters coursing down an ancient St. Croix River to the Mississippi River.

Minnesota's Vegetation

Three of North America's biomes—groups of plants and animals representing major climate zones—converge in Minnesota. This is unusual for a nonmountainous state and accounts for the diverse ecological communities, according to the state's natural resources experts. The regions are the coniferous, or boreal, forests, the deciduous forests, and the prairie grasslands.

Coniferous Forests

Located in the northeastern portion of the state, this biome mainly has evergreen trees, which grow seeds in cones. Evergreens were the dominant trees before European settlement, but after extensive logging at the turn of the 20th century, aspen and other hardwoods became a bigger part of the ecosystem. Spruce, fir, pines, and cedars can still be found, along with birch and lichens. Beneath the forest canopy, shrubs include beaked hazel, mountain maple, honeysuckle, and dogwood. The forest floor is home to an immense variety of mosses, wildflowers, and herbaceous plants. This area has both the highest—Eagle Mountain—and lowest—Lake Superior—points in the state. When Minnesotans say they're going "Up North," this is where they're headed.

The area also contains bogs and fens—wetlands that form upon layers of dead and decaying plant material called peat. Water is at or near the surface. Rain and snow are the only sources of water for bogs, which are carpeted with sphagnum moss. They are low in nutrients and acidic. These conditions make it difficult for many plants to grow, although bogs have unusual plants like pitcher plants, which trap and digest insects. Fens receive water from both precipitation and groundwater. They typically have more nutrients than bogs and are only slightly acidic. Reeds, sedges, and grasses are common in fens, which also occur in the prairie regions of the state.

Minnesota has 20 percent of the world's calcareous fens, an extremely rare type of fen that is rich in calcium.

Fun Facts from the Minnesota Department of Natural Resources (DNR)

"Conifers are well-adapted to the cool, moist northern Minnesota climate. Because they don't drop their leaves in fall, they can start photosynthesizing food right away at spring thaw—a big advantage in a place with a relatively short growing season. Their needles have a relatively small surface area and a special protective surface. Both features help prevent them from drying out in winter when there is little moisture in the air.

"With more than 6 million acres, Minnesota has more peatlands than any other state except Alaska. Because Minnesota's peatlands are rare, relatively undisturbed, and important for scientific research, more than 170,000 acres across the northern half of the state were permanently protected in 1991." (www.dnr.state.mn.us)

Deciduous Forests

The deciduous forest runs from the northwestern to the southeastern corner of the state. Deciduous trees drop their leaves each year. This forest once contained large numbers of oak, maple, and basswood. Early settlers called this 2-million-acre maple and basswood forest The Big Woods. Farming and development have dramatically changed much of the region, but pockets remain.

Many different kinds of trees grow here, depending on what kind of soil exists and how much it's been disturbed. Along the prairie edge, oaks may predominate. Where rivers run through, water-loving cottonwoods abound.

Glaciers formed most of the region's landscape, including moraines, the Mississippi River valley and its sand plain outwash, and the St. Croix River with its valley, kames, and kettle lakes. The land here is at or southeast of the line of hills, ridges, and other features created by the edge of the last glacier. This vast ice sheet didn't reach into the southeastern corner of the state, however. Geologists call glacial debris drift, and because this area didn't receive any, it's called Minnesota's "driftless" area. The geology here features caves, ravines, and sinkholes, with clear, spring-fed trout streams coursing through the steep and hilly countryside.

Prairie Grasslands

At one time, vast grasslands spread from the northwestern to the southeastern ends of the state. These grasslands ranged from sparsely vegetated sand dunes to vast fields of big bluestem up to 8 feet tall; from low, wet sedge meadows to short-grass prairies high on the bluffs of the Mississippi River. The most notable characteristic of this biome is the lack of trees; however, a wide variety of grasses and wildflowers grow here.

With the advent of European settlement, much of the flat and fertile prairie was turned into farmland. Now, just a century and a half later, only 1 percent—about 150,000 acres—of the original 18 million acres of prairie remains.

The prairie grasslands are the driest biome in the state, but moisture levels determine the types of plant communities that develop. Dry prairies contain little bluestem, side-oats grama, and porcupine grasses. Dotted blazing star, pasqueflower, and puccoons are characteristic forbs, or flowering plants. Where the frequency and intensity of fire in the dry prairie are lower, species such as bur oak and northern pin oak may invade successfully to create a community called dry oak savanna, in which gnarled and spreading bur oaks dot typical dry prairie vegetation. Most oak savannas have been lost.

In mesic prairies, moderate soil moisture supports grasses up to 6 feet tall. Big bluestem, Indian grass, and prairie dropseed generally predominate. Heart-leaved Alexander, Maximilian sunflower, and wood lily are typical flowering plants. These rich prairies occur mainly in southern and western Minnesota on level or gently rolling land.

Wet prairies occur in flat or low-lying areas with poorly drained, inorganic soils. Prairie cordgrass, blue-joint, bog reed-grass, and big bluestem dominate wet prairies, along with sedge. Wet prairies occur throughout the prairie zone but are especially common on the broad, poorly drained flats of the Glacial Lake Agassiz in Minnesota's far northwestern corner.

The calcareous seepage fen is a rare kind of prairie wetland, dominated by plants such as prairie sedge, sterile sedge, and tussock sedge. These plants have adapted to soils that are continuously saturated with cold groundwater, specifically groundwater that has been percolating through a permeable layer of porous material surfaces where this layer is exposed on a slope. Where the cold, oxygen-poor groundwater emerges, organic matter decomposes very slowly. A layer of peat accumulates, and can eventually become more than 2 feet deep. Certain very rare plant species occur only in calcareous fens. These include hair-like beak rush and beaked spike rush, specifically adapted to the water's cold temperature, high pH, and uniquely high calcium and magnesium bicarbonate content calcareous fens occur sporadically throughout much of the prairie zone in Minnesota.

More Fun Facts from the DNR

"Three major forces created and sustain prairie grasslands. First, fire suppressed trees and shrubs while stimulating the growth of prairie wildflowers and grasses. Second, prairie plants adapted to grazing by bison and other large plant eaters. Many prairie plants have underground growing points that quickly sprout after being eaten. Finally, prairie plants are adapted to drought. Many become dormant during a drought and begin growing again after the drought ends. Others have deep, thick roots that absorb nearly all available water. Some roots may be three times longer than the plants above them." (www.dnr.state.mn.us)

Minnesota's Human History

As in most of the world, Minnesota's human history begins with ancient peoples. State archaeologists have found evidence of cultures thousands of years old along Minnesota's rivers and lakes. In recorded historical times, the Dakota people lived in the north.

In the mid-1600s, French explorers arrived. Pierre Esprit Radisson and Médard des Groseilliers probably were the first white people to reach the northwestern shore of Lake Superior. Native Americans began trading furs for European goods. Trader and explorer Pierre Gaultier, Sieur de la Vérendrye, built a post on Lake of the Woods in 1732 to start the voyageur era.

As settlement pushed native people from the eastern United States, the Ojibwe arrived in the western Great Lakes. The Dakota already were moving toward the Great Plains, but conflicts with the Ojibwe pushed them south and west. After the French and Indian War ended in 1763, the French gave up their lands east of the Mississippi River, and the British took over the fur trade. Even after the American Revolution, it took a number of years for the British to leave what was then an isolated wilderness. The French still claimed the area west of the Mississippi until 1803, when it was sold to the United States in the Louisiana Purchase. Finally, the British moved their North West Company from Grand Portage into Canada.

To protect American interests, in 1820 construction began on a fort on a high bluff where the Mississippi and Minnesota rivers meet in present-day St. Paul. As European settlement spread through the state, Ojibwe and Dakota hunting and food-gathering lands vanished. Beginning in 1830, both groups signed numerous treaties giving up land. By 1851, the Dakota were confined to a reservation 10 miles either side of the Minnesota River in exchange for money, goods, and services. With land opened for settlement, immigrants from Germany, Sweden, and Norway flooded into Minnesota Territory. From 1855 to 1857, the white population nearly quadrupled. Minnesota became the 32nd state admitted to the union in 1858.

Frustration with late payments combined with crop failures and other circumstances in 1862, and the Dakota attempted to regain their land in the US–Dakota War. It's estimated that more than 600 settlers, soldiers, and Dakota people were killed in the fighting.

While homesteaders were flooding into other parts of Minnesota, iron ore was discovered in several areas in the northeastern part of the state. Ore was shipped to Duluth, then on to ships bound for the East Coast steel mills. High-grade iron ore began to run out in the 1950s, but lower-grade formations continue to be processed.

The Indian land-cession treaties also opened land for logging, and the lumber industry headed west as great eastern forests were cut and milled. Starting from east-central Minnesota in a triangle between the St. Croix and Mississippi rivers to Mille Lacs Lake, loggers moved northward. The legend of Paul Bunyan and his blue ox Babe grew out of lumberjacks' own storytelling. By 1914, most of the state's biggest trees were gone, and the industry dwindled.

Wheat had become a major crop by the 1850s, and Minneapolis had characteristics that would make it a major market and milling center by the 1870s. St. Anthony Falls provided water power, and developing railroads made Minneapolis–St. Paul a hub that reached into all corners of the state. All these industries survive in some form or number today.

Hiking Venues

Minnesotans love the outdoors. Hey, the snowmobile and the water ski were invented here. The state has a large number of well-developed and well-maintained outdoor recreation areas. Minnesota also boasts one of the nation's most pristine regions, the Boundary Waters Canoe Area Wilderness.

State Parks

The second oldest system in the United States, Minnesota has 71 state parks and recreation areas. More than 8 million people, about 20 percent from outside the state, visit each year. Parks vary from wilderness areas, where development is kept to a minimum, to sites with many recreational facilities. Most trails are easy to follow, but how well they're marked varies greatly. Some parks have named trails with well-marked intersections. Others offer only minimal guidance.

Extensive information on Minnesota's state parks is available at the Minnesota DNR web site. (www.dnr.state.mn.us/state_parks)

Vehicle permits are required for entrance. An annual permit cost $25 for one vehicle and $18 if you buy a second one. People who qualify for handicapped vehicle permits can get them for $12 per year. A daily state park vehicle permit cost $7.

Semimodern campsites at state parks cost $15 a night. Sites with electricity are $19. Rustic sites cost $11, and backpack sites are $7. A reservation fee of $8.50 is charged.

Parks reserve some sites for walk-in campers, but reservations are recommended. Call 1-866-85PARKS or go online at www.stayatmnparks.com.

Camper cabins, rustic 12- by 16-foot log cabins, can be reserved a year in advance. Most are available April through late fall. Cabins don't have running water or indoor bathrooms. Some have electricity and/or heat. Cabins without electricity are $35 per night. Those with electricity are $39 nightly. Other lodging, like guest cabins, is available and prices vary.

While leashed pets are allowed in state parks and on trails, they aren't allowed in lodging facilities.

State Forests

Hundreds of miles of trails have been built in Minnesota's 58 state forests, although they're generally less well marked than in state parks. Trail maps are available, and information on individual state forests can be found on the Minnesota Department of Natural Resources website, www.dnr.state.mn.us. Be aware that hunting is allowed in many state forests, so plan accordingly.

State forest campgrounds operate on the first-come, first-served basis. There are no facilities like flush toilets or showers. Cost is $10 per night. Registration and payment is made using envelopes at the campgrounds.

National Forests

National forests were created in 1891 to protect the country's timber supply. Conservationists, including President Teddy Roosevelt, were worried that the supply soon would be gone. Forests were defined as crops that were planted, tended, and then harvested. Today, 154 national forests cover 200 million acres in 44 states. The U.S. Forest Service uses "a vegetative management practice called clear-cutting," harvesting trees to allow young seedlings to grow. Don't be surprised if you see trucks hauling cut logs.

National forests also have been maintained as recreational areas and include hundreds of miles of hiking trails. Minnesota has two national forests. Hunting is allowed on national forest lands, so be aware while hiking during the various seasons.

Chippewa National Forest

Located in north-central Minnesota, the Chippewa National Forest has over 150 miles of hiking trails. Administrative districts, where you can get information and maps, are located in Blackduck, Cass Lake, Deer River, Marcell, and Walker. The North Country Trail, which eventually will run through seven states, also runs through this forest.

There are 380 backpacking campsites, and 23 developed campgrounds. Fees for the developed campgrounds range from $12 to $20. The Chippewa National Forest web site is www.fs.fed.us/r9/chippewa.

Superior National Forest

This national forest covers much of northeastern Minnesota, from Duluth to the Canadian border to the shore of Lake Superior. Hiking trails abound, and a wealth of information is available at district ranger stations. They are located in Tofte, Grand Marais, Ely, Aurora, and Cook. The employees have never been anything less than friendly, helpful, and informative. We never found a single question they couldn't answer, usually from memory.

There are several camping options in Superior National Forest. Developed campgrounds are available, with fees varying from $8 to $17. Backcountry sites, each with a tent pad, fire ring, and "outhouse without the house" have been developed. You actually can camp anywhere in the national forest, but using developed sites is encouraged.

The Boundary Waters Canoe Area Wilderness (BWCAW) is within Superior National Forest. *National Geographic* magazine named this one of the 50 places to visit before you die. Covering more than 1 million acres, the Boundary Waters is one of the most heavily used wilderness areas in the United States. Because of this, visitors are required to enter through specific points, and permits are issued to control how many people enter each day. It's best to check out the web site at www.bwcaw.org when planning a trip.

A huge storm on July 4, 1999–called the Big Blowdown–felled trees in over 350,000 acres of the Superior National Forest, mostly in the Boundary Waters. All these downed trees have the potential to start wildfires, so pay close attention to fire restrictions and be particularly careful. Downed or weakened trees may produce other hazards. To reduce the danger of wildfires, the Forest Service is sometimes burning downed trees. There are a limited number of days each year with the right conditions for prescribed burning, so be aware of the possibility.

Day users must fill out registration forms at trailheads. Anyone camping overnight is required to get a permit from an official issuing station. The overnight user fee is $10 per adult per trip. Seniors and people under age 17 paid $5. A reservation fee, $12, also is charged. Permit reservations can be made online at www.bwcaw.org, by calling 1-877-550-6777, or by mailing a request to BWCAW Reservation Center, P.O. Box 462, Ballston Spa, NY 12020. Again, use the web site to plan your visit.

National Park Service

Voyageurs National Park is known for its water, but there are hiking trails here as well. Thirteen hiking trails range from 0.25 to 9.5 miles in length. Some trails can be reached by land, but six are accessible only by water. You also need a boat to camp in the park. The park has three entry points. The Kabetogama Lake and Ash River Visitor Centers operate from May 14 through September 30. The Rainy Lake Visitor Center is open throughout the year. Information is available online at www.nps.gov/voya.

Pipestone and Grand Portage National Monuments also have hiking trails, and trails are located in many places along the St. Croix National Scenic Riverway and the Mississippi National River and Recreation Area. The National Park Service website, www.nps.gov, has specific information on all these areas.

Long-Distance Hiking

Many Minnesotans are willing to donate their time and talents to help others enjoy the state's natural resources. Because of this generous attitude, Minnesota has terrific long-distance hiking trails—in many cases planned, promoted, built, and maintained by volunteers.

Superior Hiking Trail

The Superior Hiking Trail runs 205 miles along the North Shore of Lake Superior—from just north of Two Harbors to the Canadian border. Much of the trail follows ridgelines inland from the lake. It weaves in and out of the numerous state parks along Minnesota's North Shore, and even travels along the shoreline for a few miles. Several hikes in this book are along the trail.

The nonprofit Superior Hiking Trail Association helped build and presently maintains the trail. Most of the route is well marked and worn, but there are spots where it can be confusing or overgrown. About 75 campsites have been built along the trail. No permits, fees, or reservations are required. They're first-come, first-served. Most campsites have space for two to four tents, but larger, multigroup sites exist. Sites have tent pads, backcountry latrines, fire rings, and benches. Most are near water. Dogs are permitted, but they have to be on leashes.

Most trailheads have parking areas. Because the trail runs in a straight line, you have to figure out how to get to or back from your hike. The association suggests several methods:

1. Hike with another person and park cars at both ends of the hike.
2. Sign up for an official association hike, and shuttle service will be included.
3. Use the Superior Shuttle van, which holds up to ten passengers and their equipment. The shuttle runs on a fixed schedule Fridays, Saturdays, and Sundays from mid-May to mid-October. Reservations are encouraged but not necessary. Scheduling a trip at another time is possible, but depends on whether a driver is available and costs more than regular service. Contact Superior Shuttle owner Dan Sanders at 218-834-5511.

The 2004 edition of *The Guide to the Superior Hiking Trail* is essential if you're going to spend much time on this trail. It shows trailheads and parking areas and gives campsite details, such as where water is available.

The association operates a store in Two Harbors, in a blue Victorian house at the corner of MN 61 and Eighth Street. Trail maps, hiking guides, trail-related merchandise, and hiking accessories are for sale. The store is open 9 AM to 5 PM Monday through Friday; 10 AM to 4 PM Saturday; and noon to 4 PM Sunday from mid-May through mid-October.

The association's mailing address is P.O. Box 4, Two Harbors, MN 55616. The e-mail address is suphike@mr.net. The telephone number is 218-834-2700. The Superior Hiking Trail Association's website is www.shta .org.

Many lodges and inns along the North Shore participate in a lodge-to-lodge hiking program. After hiking, you stay at a lodge or inn where you receive overnight lodging, breakfast, and a lunch for the trail. After breakfast you drive your vehicle and gear to the spot you'll end up, then you're shuttled back to the start of the trail section to begin your hike. You could also use the Superior Shuttle. The Superior Hiking Trail Association can provide information about which lodging establishments have lodge-to-lodge services.

Kekekabic Trail

The Kekekabic Trail, constructed in the 1930s, is a former access route for firefighters and forest management employees. This rugged, 40-mile trail runs from the end of the Fernberg Road east of Ely near Snowbank Lake to the Gunflint Trail. The trail ends across a road from the start of the Border Route Trail.

The western portion of the trail has campsites for hikers. It takes four to six days to hike the entire trail, which is difficult to follow in some areas. Clear-cutting wiped out parts of the trail near its west end, but these spots are being reestablished. Flagging tape marks the route in some areas. Water also is unavailable for long stretches, so you have to carry your own. BWCAW regulations apply on the sections of trail within its boundary.

The Kekekabic Trail Club maintains the route every year. The club's web site is www.kek.org. Their e-mail address is info@ kek.org.

Border Route Trail

This is a rugged backpacking trail that follows the Canadian border through the Superior National Forest, along ridgelines and high cliffs. More than half of the 75-mile route is in the Boundary Waters Canoe Area Wilderness. At its west end, the trail meets the Kekekabic Trail. On its east end, it connects to the Superior Hiking Trail. Access is from the Gunflint or Arrowhead Trails. Most of the trail is maintained. Spur and connecting trails also can be used to plan day hikes. Grand Marais and Hovland are the closest towns.

Most BWCAW campsites are for canoeists, but hikers can use them. Refer to the BWCAW section for information about getting permits required for overnight camping. Outside the BWCAW, National Forest rules apply. You can camp anywhere, but using established campsites is preferable and encouraged. Be aware that the Border Route Trail has long sections with no water sources.

The Minnesota Rovers Outing Club, Minnesota Department of Natural Resources, and the U.S. Forest Service built the trail. The club, which publishes a guidebook, maintains it. The *Border Route Trail Guide* contains detailed topographic maps, campsite information, and the history of areas along the trail. "Because of its rugged and primitive nature, the trail provides solitude and a true wilderness experience but also requires good map and compass skills," according to the club. Contact the group at 651-257-7324 or visit their web site at www.mnrovers.org.

The Border Route Trail website is www.borderroutetrail.org.

North Country Trail

The North Country National Scenic Trail, a unit of the National Park Service, will run more than 4,000 miles across seven northern states. More than 1,700 miles have been certified off-road. Additional miles follow shared footpaths, but some road walks remain. It will be the longest off-road hiking trail in the United States. National headquarters is in Lowell, Michigan, near the geographic center of the trail.

In Minnesota, the trail runs from near Walker to near Remer, with the longest section in the Chippewa National Forest. The National Park Service was taking public comments on the trail in late 2004. The web site is www.northcountrytrail.org.

Hiking Specifics

Day hiking is less complicated than backpacking trips, however, there are several essential requirements. Footwear is the most important consideration. Every hiker has a strong opinion about shoes vs. boots, leather vs. synthetics, ankle-high vs. lowriders. Obviously, it's a personal matter, but we'd like to caution against shoes that don't fit or are uncomfortable. Nothing ruins a hike more than getting a mile down the trail and realizing that your boot is rubbing your ankle bone raw. The same goes for socks. Get professional advice in picking out footwear, and don't skimp to save a few bucks if it doesn't feel right.

The next essential ingredient is common sense, and we think that handles just about everything else. Plan ahead. Don't know the area you're heading to? Bring a map. Know the trails aren't well marked? Bring a compass. At your hiking speed, the route will take most of the day? Bring food. The weather report says it's going to be 90 degrees? Bring plenty of water. Weather forecast predicts rain? Bring your wet weather gear. Forecast predicts thunderstorms? Maybe you should postpone your trip.

Most guides caution against hiking alone, but Gwen confesses to craving the solitude of a solo hike. Whatever you do, let someone know where you're going and how long you can expect to be gone. Even if a hike isn't in a wilderness area, it can be a long way back to civilization if you're hurt. If you're seriously injured, trying to hike back may not even be an option.

Even day hikers need to tread lightly and leave no trace. The U.S. Forest Service has come up with these guidelines:

- Pack it in, pack it out.
- Properly dispose of anything you can't remove.
- Leave the land as you found it.
- In popular places, concentrate use.
- In pristine places, disperse use.
- Avoid places that are lightly worn or just beginning to show signs of use.
- Keep noise to a minimum and strive to be inconspicuous.

The Hikes in This Book

We have organized these hikes based on the three major biomes used by the Department of Natural Resources plus the Mississippi River bluffs, which is a unique geological area of the state.

We have described the hikes as we found them, but sometimes signs fall down, trails become damaged, and closed sections of trail get repaired. Occasionally, signs or benches that people told us to look for weren't there. On other trails, markers had become hidden as vegetation grew. We noticed them after backtracking and coming from a new angle.

We judged a hike's difficulty in comparison to the "easy," "more difficult," and "most difficult" system commonly used in state parks. When there was a question about mileage, we deferred to official sources—be they maps or park employees.

Your hiking speed also may differ from ours. How fast people walk depends on heat, humidity, rainfall, the amount of sleep you got the night before, and whether you're coming down with a cold. For example, five days we spent hiking along the North Shore of Lake Superior in August turned out to be during one of the hottest, most humid weeks of summer. The normally cool, refreshing air was dense. About 10 minutes into every hike, we were wringing wet. If the weather had been cooler, we would have moved faster.

So given all that, we probably hike at a rate similar to most people. Only once were we passed by a young man loaded with equipment on the Superior Hiking Trail, who was clipping along as if he had a deadline to meet.

Coniferous Forests

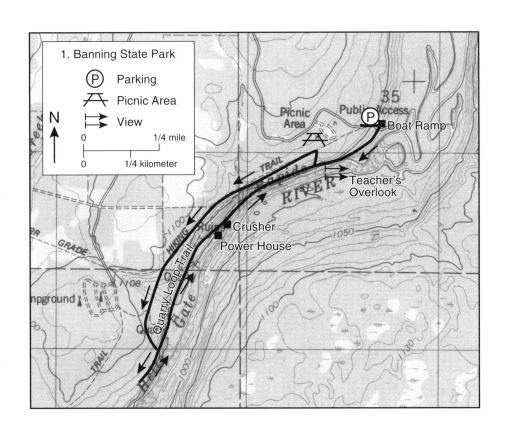

1

Banning State Park

Total distance: 3 miles

Approximate hiking time: 1.5 hours

Difficulty: Easy with some moderate spots

Vertical rise: 100 feet

Maps: USGS 7½' Sandstone North quad, Minnesota Department of Natural Resources state park map

Banning State Park is named for a town that doesn't exist anymore. A sandstone quarry was developed along the Kettle River in the early 1890s, employing about 500 people and sprouting nearby villages.

Logging was another important industry in the area, and nearby Hinckley was a railroad hub that served the logging and stone industries. A catastrophic fire in September 1894, fueled by large piles of waste timber, killed 400 people in Hinckley, burned 500 square miles, and disrupted area businesses.

Despite the fire, the quarry resumed operation. A village was drawn out above the quarry in 1896, and by the turn of the 20th century, 300 people lived there. The hamlet was named for William L. Banning, a Pennsylvania native and banker who served in Minnesota's Third Regiment during the Civil War and became president of the St. Paul–Duluth Railroad.

The town's life was short, because structural steel soon became preferred for constructing buildings. By 1912, the town of Banning had vanished. On this hike, you walk by all that remains of the quarry's buildings.

The sandstone that gave birth to the quarry and Banning is related to the volcanic activity that formed the North Shore bedrock billions of years ago. As the molten magma rose, it created a low area in the vicinity of Lake Superior. The tan to buff-colored sandstone, called Hinckley sandstone, may have formed in a basin lake where streams continued to bring in water and sediment.

The Kettle River

The debris left by melting glaciers is shallow throughout the park. Bedrock is exposed all along the Kettle River, which is part of the National Wild and Scenic Rivers program. The river's name refers to the water-worn holes in the riverbank's rock. Swirling water turns sand or tiny pebbles round and round, and a depression is carved. As the kettle gets bigger, more sand, pebbles, and rocks are caught, acting as grinders to further enlarge the hole.

The park's original vegetation was red and white pine. Logging and forest fires resulted in second growth of aspen and birch, with remnants of the pine woods. In spring, trillium and bloodroot can be seen blooming, and mosses and ferns are common along the rocks and cliff faces.

The 6,237-acre park has 33 semimodern campsites, ten of which have electricity. Four canoe campsites are available, and the park has three small boat landings. A camper cabin, with no heat or electricity, can also be rented.

As the Kettle River flows southward, it tumbles over a series of rapids into a gorge worn through the sandstone. These rapids are a popular attraction for canoeists and kayakers. The park's telephone number is 320-245-2668.

How to Get There

Sandstone is about 80 miles north of Minneapolis on I-35. From Sandstone, head approximately 4 miles northeast on MN 23 to the park's entrance. Turn south on the park road, and drive southeast to the parking area for the picnic area and boat ramp.

The Trail

Park in the lot for the boat ramp, and walk about 0.1 mile to the river. Turn right onto a

Coniferous Forests

grass path that passes the first rapids, named the Blueberry Slide. Continue downriver and over a boardwalk. Spur trails lead down to the broad, flat bedrock along the river, where you can check out the kettles. As you near the picnic area, the official and unofficial trails, to your right up the bank, can be confusing. To get to the main trail for this hike, keep heading up. Look for an area with picnic tables called the Teacher's Overlook. Just north of this spot is a kiosk with holders for self-guided trail maps. It was empty the day we hiked, so you might want to plan ahead and stop at the park's information office.

Follow the Quarry Loop Trail. The loop begins in about 0.1 mile, and we went counterclockwise on the higher part. After about 0.3 mile, you pass the Cartway Trail to your right, then cross a bridge over a stream that was dry the day we visited. On this part of the trail, you pass rocky outcrops amid the birch, aspen, and shrubs.

The next intersection is with the Township Trail, then an intersection with the Spur Trail follows a few paces afterward. Continue on the Quarry Loop Trail.

The trail descends in switchbacks, and the sandstone cliff rises to your right. You come to a smooth area of rock wall that was quarried. The next trail to your right is the Deadman Trail, which has nothing to do with a deceased human. In a quarry, a deadman is an anchor set in the ground to support cables for derricks that lift stone onto carts or railroad cars.

Continue straight ahead. The trail curves to your left and passes sandstone blocks left over from the quarry.

At the intersection with the Hell's Gate Trail, turn right. This trail becomes a narrow dirt path that hugs the river for about 0.3 mile. You pass the Hell's Gate Rapids, down a few steep inclines, under a rock overhang, around boulders, and over a fallen tree—all while trying not to fall into the Kettle River and hugging the cliff. This spur trail ends with a lovely scene of a rocky outcrop in the river. Turn around, and retrace your steps back to the Quarry Loop.

Follow the Quarry Loop Trail to your right. The trail passes what remains of the quarry, including a stone-cutting shed, a power-house, and a building where rocks too small to be used for construction were crushed for cement mix and railroad grades.

Continue past an intersection with the Spur Trail to your left. The trail starts to rise above the river and its Dragon's Tooth Rapids, as you pass through birch and pine. Look for a post with the number 17, where you head to the left up stone steps. A bench sits at the top, and signs mark MCC and Hiking Club trails.

To get back to the boat ramp parking area, you have two choices here. You can continue on the Quarry Loop Trail to the picnic area, then follow the park road east, to your right. The second option is to follow the MCC Trail back down to the river, retracing your steps along the grassy bank to the boat ramp, then walking west, to your left, up the road to the parking lot.

2

Bear Head Lake State Park

Total distance: 4.2 miles

*Approximate hiking time: 2 hours,
30 minutes*

Difficulty: Moderate

Vertical rise: 50 feet

*Maps: USGS 7½' Eagles Nest quad,
Minnesota Department of Natural
Resources state park map*

Bear Head Lake State Park is a comeback kid among state parks. First, the area was logged heavily beginning in the late 1890s. The local Tower Lumber Company began operating on Bear Head Lake, producing timber needed to support the mining industry. The nationwide gold fever struck in northern Minnesota with rumors of precious metals among the ancient rocks.

The area's greenstone belts may have lured prospectors. After volcanic activity stopped in ancient Minnesota, the underlying rocks experienced intense folding. Underlying granite began rising through the volcanic rock and interspersed sedimentary layers, raising their temperature and changing them. Some of the minerals in the dark gray to black basalts were changed to green minerals and commonly called greenstone, which sometimes contain gold, silver, copper, nickel, and zinc.

However, the area around Lake Vermilion, northeast of the park, yielded precious metal of another sort—iron ore. At first the high-grade ore was mined in open pits. As the pit walls became steeper, they needed bracing as underground shafts were dug. Lumber also was needed to build homes in the Tower-Soudan area.

So a local timber industry sprang up. The Tower Lumber Company acquired a small railroad and used "portage" lines to haul logs from one lake to another. By 1911, the prime forest around Bear Head Lake had been used up, and lumber operations ended.

Then for the next two years, fires consumed most of whatever trees were left

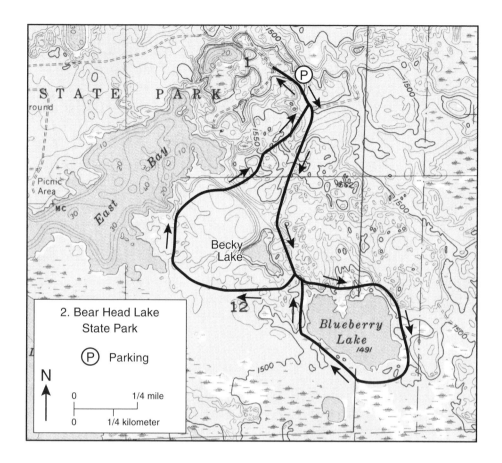

2. Bear Head Lake
State Park

P Parking

N

0   1/4 mile

0   1/4 kilometer

within the park's boundaries. Charred stumps remain.

Today, a second-growth forest of deciduous hardwoods and pine covers the park's terrain, hills formed when glaciers moved over the Ely greenstone and Giants Range granite bedrock. Bear Head Lake sits in a greenstone depression. On a map, the lower part of the lake looks like a bear growling with its mouth open.

Most of the camping, swimming, and picnic facilities at this 4,000-acre park are clustered around Bear Head Lake's North Bay, leaving the eastern section of park wild and undeveloped. The campground has 73 semimodern sites, 26 with electricity, and modern rest rooms and showers. The less-developed area has four hike-in campsites, one boat-accessible site, and a primitive group camp. A guest house and one camper cabin, with screen porch, heat, electricity, and nearby flush toilets and showers, can be rented. A trailer sanitation station also is available. Contact the park by calling 218-365-7229.

How to Get There

From Tower, which is about 25 miles north of Virginia, head northeast on US 169, passing through Soudan, for about 18 miles. Turn south onto St. Louis County 128 and drive approximately 6 miles to the park entrance.

The Becky Lake Trail

The Trail

This hike starts from a parking area on a road marked "authorized vehicles only." If you're coming from the park entrance, look for a park sign indicating group and backpack camping to your left. If you've stopped at the park office, look for the gated road—open during park hours—just past the Norberg Lake Trail parking area.

Continue past the primitive camp road to the parking area. The trail starts at a wooden post with a NO PARKING sign. Walk a short distance on an old gravel road to the signpost at the start of the Becky Lake Trail loop. From where you stand, both trails lead out in a V. Head down the left-hand path. The trail is narrow and rocky in spots with moderate ascents and descents. A number of trees also were down over the trail on our last visit. At about 0.8 mile, pass a marker for the first backpack campsite, on Becky Lake.

At 0.9 mile is an intersection with a sign reading Blueberry Lake Trail. Head to your left, and shortly you come to an intersection with a mapboard attached to a tree. Head left again. The narrow footpath was overgrown slightly by the end of summer when we hiked. The trail includes several steep, but short, ascents and descents as you continue around the lake. You pass spur trails to campsites 2 and 3 on the shore. You can't see if anyone is camping until you get close, but we ventured down quietly. The sites were empty and provided nice views of Blueberry Lake.

Now the main trail, marked with blue diamonds, ascends slightly and passes through an area of red pine. Continue around the south end of the lake, past campsite 4, and through a low, wet area. The trail is mostly level as you head back to the start of the Blueberry Lake loop.

Turn left at the loop intersection, then left again at the Blueberry Lake Trail sign. Becky Lake is to your right through the trees. Pass through tall stands of jack and red pine.

Coniferous Forests

About 0.6 mile past the Blueberry Lake Trail sign is a park shelter with a short trail to the shore of Bear Head Lake's East Bay. Just steps further down the main trail is a spur leading to campsite 5.

The trail stays near the lake for another 0.3 mile, then turns east and continues in moderate ascents and descents. This section of trail is used for cross-country skiing and is a little less rugged than the Blueberry Lake loop. Continue for about 0.6 mile to the Becky Lake sign at the old road. Turn left to the parking area.

Bonus Destination

Iron ore was discovered at the site of Soudan Underground Mine State Park in 1865, but it wasn't until 1884 that the first shipment ever produced in Minnesota left the mine. Minnesota's famous Iron Range was born.

The Vermilion Range ores, named after the lake where they first were discovered, originated during Minnesota's ancient volcanic period. Volcanic vents and fissures exhaled iron, silicon, and other elements into hot waters. Under the right chemical conditions, the iron came out as thin bands of hematite, magnetite, siderite, pyrite, or iron silicate.

At first, the Soudan ore was gathered from seven open pits, in which miners used ropes to move around the walls. About 1892, miners discovered that the ore body went almost straight into the ground. Underground shafts and tunnels became necessary. Eventually, the shaft extended 2,500 feet underground, with tunnels running 0.75 mile off the central core.

The Soudan mine was the largest of 11 in the Vermilion Range and employed 1,800 miners at the height of production. The mine's general manager named the town because the severe winters here contrasted with the tropical heat of the Sudan region of Africa. Before it closed in 1962, the Soudan mine had yielded 14 million metric tons of ore.

US Steel sold the site to the State of Minnesota in 1963. Visitors can ride the shaft elevator, called "the cage," to the mine's 27th level. Drilling and blasting equipment sits where it was abandoned. An underground railroad car then travels to the last area the miners worked. Above-ground, buildings have been preserved, and displays and exhibits explain the mine's history. This unique state park is a National Historic Landmark.

The town of Soudan is located 22 miles southwest of Ely. The park is open daily Memorial Day through Labor Day. An admission fee is charged.

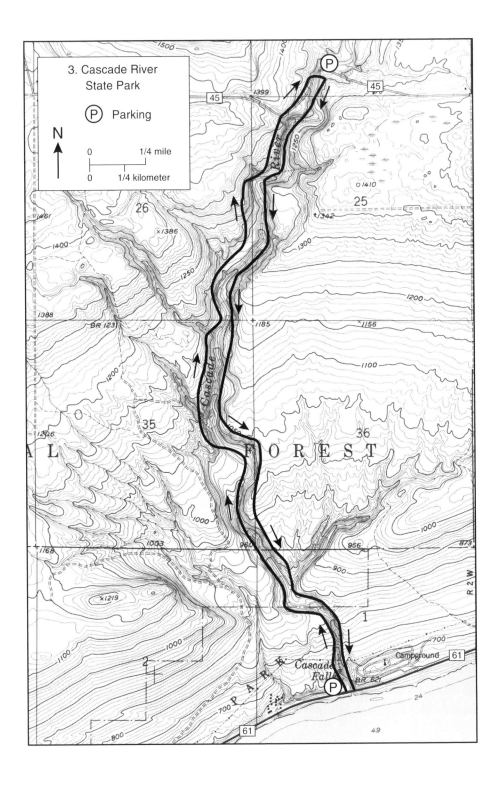

3. Cascade River
State Park

P Parking

N

0   1/4 mile
0   1/4 kilometer

3

Cascade River State Park

Total distance: 7.8 miles

Approximate hiking time: 5 hours

Difficulty: Moderate to difficult

Vertical rise: 1,000 feet

Maps: USGS 7½' Deer Yard Lake quad, Minnesota Department of Natural Resources state park map

The North Shore doesn't lack waterfalls; 22 major streams cut through rock gorges and tumble over ledges and boulders of various sizes. Yet each river or stream has its own personality or attraction.

It's easy to understand how this river got its name. The river flows down a series of ledges, dropping 900 feet in its last 3 miles as it flows through a twisting gorge near Lake Superior. The Cascade River starts in an area of many lakes, marshes, and ponds, ensuring that the faucet is always turned on for its waterfalls.

The park's geology, like that of the entire North Shore, is ancient. About 1.2 billion years ago, North America began to split. Lava began flowing up through the cracks in hundreds of individual flows. Eventually, the layers of thick molten rock caused the underlying area to sink. Later eruptions tilted the previous flows, and layers of sandstone that formed in between, toward the center of the basin that became Lake Superior.

Glacial drift is thin or nonexistent along the North Shore, and rock outcrops are the dominant landscape feature. Indeed, one book on the state's geology calls the North Shore "one mass rock outcrop." The park has a picnic area along the lake, south of US 61, where you can explore the North Shore's tilted shoreline strewn with gray boulders.

Before the area became a state park in 1957, the Civilian Conservation Corps operated a riverside camp. As in many such camps, men built trails and other structures. They even cut and moved large logs south

Waterfalls on the Cascade River

to Gooseberry Falls State Park for building construction there.

The forest here is a mix of boreal hardwood and conifer. Birch and spruce are common, along with fir and aspen. White cedar is found in moist areas. Along the river gorge, moss and ferns grow in the moist climate.

The park has 18 miles of hiking and cross-country skiing trails and a year-round trail center building with a wood stove. The semimodern campground has 40 sites, showers, flush toilets, and trailer sanitation facilities. A primitive group camp and five hike-in campsites also are available. The phone number is 218-387-3053.

How to Get There

Cascade River State Park is about 98 miles north of Duluth. From Tofte, drive 21 miles northeast on US 61. The park entrance is right on the road and well marked with state highway and colorful park signs.

The Trail

This is a long hike with steep, rocky, and root-covered sections. The terrain drops steeply from the trail in several places. In wet weather, footing can be treacherous.

Park in the trail center lot, along the western edge of the campground loops. The trailhead is to the north and marked with Cascade River Trail, Superior Hiking Trail, and Hiking Club signs. Follow the trail up and down stone steps and turn left to the bridge. Here you have a view of several lower cascades. Turn right onto the Superior Hiking Trail. Pass by a trail intersection to your left, staying toward the river. Walk down 96 steps. You can walk right down to the large, flat expanse of rock through which the river flows. Decaying material in swamps and bogs upriver, as well as iron deposits, give the water its brown color.

Continue upriver. Along this section, the trail rises about 100 feet over 0.5 mile and sticks next to the river.

About 1.4 miles from the start of this hike comes a spur trail that leads to a waterfall in a tributary of the Cascade. It's 0.3 mile to the waterfall, then you retrace your steps back to the Superior Hiking Trail. The main trail goes to your left and heads away from the river. Cross a bridge over a small stream where the trail turns to your right, and you pass the Big White Pine campsite.

Cross another bridge, and the trail begins a steep ascent. After crossing a 25-foot bridge, you come to the Cut Log campsite to your left. The site is named for white pine logs, one nearly 4 feet across, left behind by loggers years ago. However, you now hike through stands of young and mature maple as the trail continues through the valley of two river tributaries.

Soon the trail turns back toward the river, and you come to a steep ascent with a collapsed riverbank. This is a very steep dropoff, so be careful.

Head up onto Cook County Road 45 and turn right. Walk about 0.2 mile, cross the river, and turn into a parking area to your left. The Superior Hiking Trail continues north, but you want to loop under the bridge to catch the trail, which leads down the other side of the river. For about the next 0.4 mile, the trail includes a fair number of rocks and the roots of old cedar trees. There also are several steep descents and ascents on wooden steps. Pass the Hidden Falls. The trail continues its ascents and descents, then enters private property for 1.5 miles. It's important that you stay on the trail here, which passes through a moist area of cedar.

Next, head up a steep section of log stairs to a ridge high above the river. Look for large white pine. You gradually descend as you walk along the river gorge. Cross-country skiing trails intersect the trail, but continue straight ahead on the Superior Hiking Trail. Pass the Trout Creek campsite to your right, then cross a bridge over the creek itself. Here you can see layered red sandstone.

The trail turns left, away from the river, and ascends a steep ridge. The trees here are spruce and birch, with a typical boreal forest floor of bunchberry and bluebead lily. Ignore the cross-country skiing trails to your left, but head down a spur trail to the right with a view back up the Cascade River.

Continuing on the main trail, you meet several trail intersections. Again, stay on the Superior Hiking Trail until you come to the bridge that leads across the Cascade River. A left turn takes you back to the trailhead parking lot. However, we went straight ahead 0.2 mile to the Lake Superior shore. As the sun set, we watched the color of the water and rocks turn to shades of orange and purple.

4

Chippewa National Forest, Shingobee Recreation Area, and North Country Trail

Total distance: 3 miles

Approximate hiking time: 1.5 hours

Difficulty: Easy to moderate

Vertical rise: 100 feet

Maps: USGS 7½' Akeley and Walker quads, USDA Forest Service map

National Forests were created in 1891 to protect the country's timber supply. When European settlers arrived in the United States, the forests seemed endless. After vast numbers of the new nation's trees were cut down for building and forests were cleared for cropland, Congress decided the resources needed to be managed. Forests were defined as crops that were planted, tended, then harvested. Today, 154 national forests cover 200 million acres in 44 states. The US Forest Service uses "a vegetative management practice called clearcutting," or harvesting trees to allow young seedlings to grow.

In 2004, the federal government unveiled long-range plans that would allow slightly more logging in nonwilderness areas of National Forests. The plan classifies about 450,000 of 675,000 acres in Chippewa National Forest as suitable for timber production and estimates that about 7,700 would be cut annually. The plan didn't please either environmental groups or the timber industry, and controversy continues.

Chippewa National Forest was the first of Minnesota's two national forests. President Teddy Roosevelt named it the Minnesota National Forest in 1908, but the name was changed to honor the area's original inhabitants in 1928. Chippewa is the Anglicized version of Ojibwe.

As in much of northern Minnesota, red and white pine once covered the area. The forests grew over the rolling hills of rock and debris deposited after the last glaciers

Recreation Lake in Shingobee Recreation Area

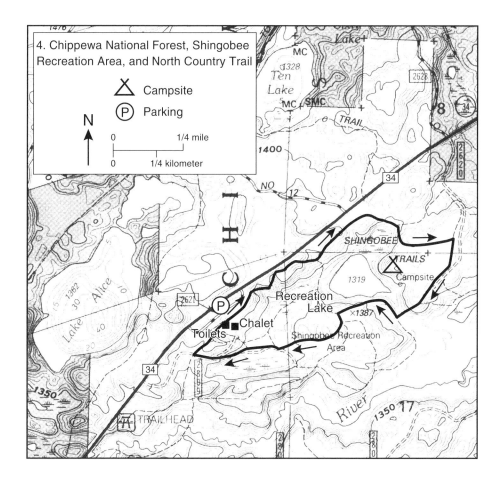

4. Chippewa National Forest, Shingobee Recreation Area, and North Country Trail

△ Campsite

Ⓟ Parking

N

0   1/4 mile

0   1/4 kilometer

melted about 10,000 years ago. Second-growth aspen and birch are interspersed with planted pine.

Chippewa National Forest also is studded with 1,321 lakes and contains 900 miles of rivers. The habitat supports white-tailed deer, black bears, porcupines, raccoons, and 230 bird species including the bald eagle. Wildflowers that bloom from spring through autumn include marsh marigolds, hepaticas, spring beauties, trillium, blue flag, jack-in-the-pulpit, columbine, and wild rose. During an early August hike, fragrant hyssop, daisy fleabane, fireweed, goldenrod, and purple asters were blooming.

Sixty-eight miles of the North Country Trail, marked with signposts, wind through Chippewa National Forest. Camping is allowed anywhere in National Forests, but about eight campsites have been cleared along this portion of the trail. The Forest Service recommends using developed campsites to minimize your impact on the land.

A good introduction to the trail is where it passes through the Shingobee Recreation Area for about 1.5 miles. Shingobee comes from the Ojibwe word *jingob,* which was used as a general term for evergreen trees, mostly cedar, spruce, and balsam. The Civilian Conservation Corps developed trails, ski slopes, and a toboggan slide in the early 1930s. It was a center for skiing through the 1940s and operated on and off as a downhill ski area until 1984. A warming chalet at the sliding hill is open during winter weekends.

The nearest National Forest district office is in Walker. The phone number is 218-547-1044.

How to Get There

Shingobee Recreation Area is about 5 miles southwest of Walker, off MN 34. Walker, on the south shore of Leech Lake, is 185 miles north of Minneapolis–St. Paul.

The Trail

From the circular parking area, head southeast, then turn to your left onto the trail, which begins a steep descent immediately. This part of the trail, which passes the sliding hill, has moderately steep ups and downs for about 0.5 mile. When you come to a trail intersection, stay to your left on a wide mowed grass path under jack pine and small aspen. At just past 0.75 mile is the intersection with the North Country Trail, where a large signboard describes the trail. Go straight ahead. At about 1 mile, another trail leads off to your left. Stay to the right on the North Country Trail. Just past 1.25 miles, turn right at a T-intersection. You pass a cleared campsite, constructed in memory of Harry Jennings Crockett, according to a large sign. Just past the campsite is an area of very tall pines on your right.

Approximately 1.5 miles from the start of this hike, the North Country Trail heads east. To stay on the Shingobee trails system, turn right. Soon you come to a marsh, and the trail continues its roller coaster ups and downs. At a T-intersection marked with a mapboard, turn right. You will see Recreation Lake through the trees to your right and ascend a ridge above the lake. A bench is available for taking in the lake view, but on the soggy day we hiked the mosquitoes were vicious.

As you near the southwestern end of Recreation Lake, you'll come to another T-intersection marked as a cross-country ski trail. Turn left. About 50 feet up the trail is another intersection; bear right here. This is an old logging road. Go straight through the next intersection, and pass through a meadow in which purple aster, goldenrod, and black-eyed Susan were blooming in August. Pass the chalet and toilets south of the sliding hill and continue another 0.1 mile, where a right turn will take you back to the parking area.

If you plan ahead and arrange transportation, you can continue on the North Country Trail where it turns east about 0.1 mile past the Harry Jennings Crockett campsite. Follow the North Country Trail sign to the left. In about 0.4 mile, you'll come to a marshy area and cross a bridge over the creek heading out of Anoway Lake. The trail then follows a high ridge along the Shingobee River, and meets County Road 50 in about 1.5 miles. Follow the road, crossing a bridge over the river, for about 0.25 mile to a parking area with a large map of the North Country Trail.

5

George H. Crosby–Manitou State Park

Total distance: 2.6 miles

Approximate hiking time: 3 hours

Difficulty: Moderate with very difficult spots

Vertical rise: 300 feet

Maps: USGS 7½' Little Marais quad, Minnesota Department of Natural Resources state park map

George H. Crosby–Manitou State Park is a hiking park. It has no developed facilities, only 21 backpacking campsites, and a walk-in picnic area along its 23 miles of trails. The wild, rugged terrain has been preserved according to the wishes of namesake Crosby, a mining executive. The town of Crosby on the Cuyuna Iron Range also honors this avid outdoorsman.

The other part of the name comes from the Manitou River, which flows northwest to southeast through the entire park. Manitou means "spirit" in Ojibwe. The river's cascades rush through rock formed by the Keweenawan lava flows and intrusions.

Like the nearby Cascade River, the Manitou's water resembles frothy root beer. Decaying organic material in the swamps and bogs that drain into the river creates humic acid, which turns the water brown. As the water churns through gorges and tumbles over rocks, it becomes aerated and foamy. And there's plenty of foam as the Manitou flows through a deep gorge whose lower section is within park boundaries.

Very old trees grow in Crosby-Manitou. Some yellow birches are 400 years old; an upland white cedar forest has 300-year-old trees.

In September 2004, a land swap that could add 1,740 acres of old-growth hardwood forest was worked out between the Parks and Trails Council of Minnesota, Lake County, and the Minnesota Department of Natural Resources (DNR). The council will hold the land along Horseshoe Ridge until the state legislature provides money, so the

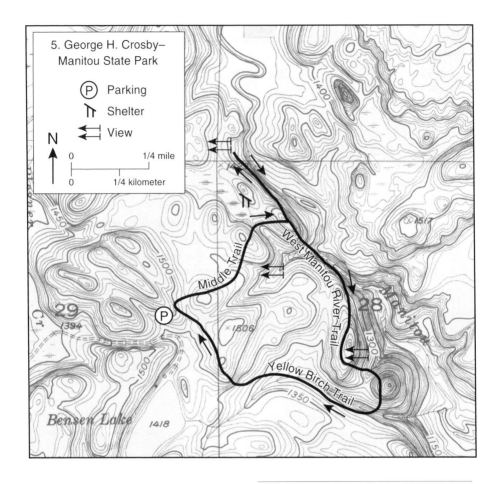

5. George H. Crosby–
Manitou State Park

Ⓟ Parking

🏠 Shelter

🔭 View

N

0   1/4 mile

0   1/4 kilometer

DNR can buy it and add it to the park. The parks council president called the ridge area "one of the most scenic and remote portions of the North Shore highlands."

Because of the park's primitive nature, black bears can be found. If bears have been sighted in the area, make noise as you hike to alert them to your presence. If you're going to camp, take precautions to discourage bears from visiting. Use rope to hang your food pack, garbage, and other items with a strong or sweet odor from a tree branch at least 10 feet off the ground. If you do encounter a bear, make noise. Most bears will be scared off.

How to Get There

From Duluth, drive northeast on US 61 for about 57 miles to Illgen City. Turn west, a left, onto MN 1 and drive 5 miles to Finland. Head north, a right turn, onto Lake County 7, for approximately 8 miles. The paved road turns to gravel past the Air Base Road, shortly before the park entrance. This park has no information office.

The Trail

This isn't a long hike, but the rugged nature of the trails makes it strenuous. We hiked during one of the summer's hottest and most humid weeks. The normally cool air of

The Cascades on the Manitou River

the North Shore was stuffy, and by the end of this hike we were tired.

The parking area is about 0.5 mile off the county road. There is a large information kiosk where campers fill out registration forms. The Middle Trail starts near the vault toilet on the parking area's north side. This section also is part of the Superior Hiking Trail. The first part of the trail is a rugged, narrow dirt path with many roots and rocks that ascends and descends gently. Next is a steeper descent to a boardwalk over a wet area, then comes a rocky incline. After about 0.3 mile is a spur trail to an overlook on your right.

The trail continues its ups and downs, passing a birch tree growing from the top of a 5-foot-wide boulder. The trees' roots have a tight grasp on the rock. About 0.5 mile from the start of this hike is a log shelter

with a fire ring. There is a Hiking Club sign here also. The Middle Trail continues to the left of the shelter.

At a T-intersection, turn left to the Cascades. The trail descends from the river gorge in a series of steep wooden steps. The trail continues past the Cascades, but after taking in the view, we climbed back up the steps, past the Middle Trail intersection, and downriver on the West River Trail. Spur trails lead to campsites 3 and 4 right on the river. Next, the trail crosses a board bridge over a stream, then ascends timber steps. The Superior Hiking Trail takes a sharp left and continues over the Manitou River.

The trail descends steeply and you cross another bridge. The next intersection is with a trail to campsites 5, 6, and 7 on your left. Head to the right on what is now the Misquah Hill Trail. Shortly, a trail to another overlook with a view of Lake Superior goes to the left.

The next intersection is with a trail that leads to more campsites down the river. The Misquah Hill trail continues to your right, then shortly comes to a T-intersection. Turn right onto the Yellow Birch Trail, which is named for the stands of these mature trees.

The trail is fairly level for the next 0.5 mile, then returns to ups and downs. A trail to Lake Bensen goes off to your left. Continue straight ahead about 0.2 mile to the parking area.

Gooseberry Falls State Park

Total distance: 2.5 miles

Approximate hiking time: 1.5 hours

Difficulty: Moderate with difficult spots

Vertical rise: 100 feet

Maps: USGS 7½' Split Rock Point quad, Minnesota Department of Natural Resources state park map

The Gooseberry River appears on explorers' maps as early as 1670. There are two versions of the name's origin. One ties it to the Ojibwe name *shab-on-im-i-kan-i-sibi*, the other to the French explorer Sieur des Groseilliers. When translated, both names refer to gooseberries.

Logging was the principal industry along the river by the late 1890s, and all the large pines were gone by the early 1920s. Stumps can be seen along trails.

At the same time, tourism began to grow along the North Shore. The Minnesota Legislature authorized preserving the Gooseberry Falls area in 1933, and Civilian Conservation Corps (CCC) workers began developing the park a year later. They built the park's beautiful buildings out of stone from a quarry southwest of Beaver Bay, and with logs, some supplied by CCC workers at the Cascade River camp farther north. The buildings are on the National Register of Historic Places. Gooseberry Falls State Park was officially designated in 1937.

The falls on the Gooseberry River are one of the most popular tourist attractions on the North Shore. However, most people stick close to the visitor center to view the Middle and Lower Falls below the MN 61 bridge. Here the layers of lava that form the North Shore spread 200 feet across in shelves, over which water tumbles to Lake Superior. A thick basalt lava flow holds up the main falls. The broad rock ledge below is a smooth flow top studded with calcite and

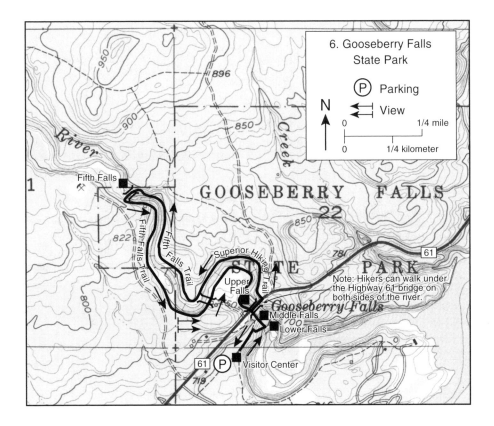

Note: Hikers can walk under the Highway 61 bridge on both sides of the river.

zeolite that filled chambers formed by gases escaping as the lava crystallized. About 30 different lava flows have been identified throughout the Gooseberry River falls.

The water flowing over the falls varies with the season. When we visited in August, the flow was gentle enough to allow sitting on the rocky ledges as the water splashed over.

This is a busy state park, with a large visitor center with interpretive displays and a nature store. The campground has 70 modern sites, three group campsites, a trailer dump station, and picnic areas. To contact the park, call 218-834-3855.

How to Get There

From Two Harbors, which is about 27 miles north of Duluth, drive 13 miles northeast on MN 61. The park entrance, on the east side of the highway, is well marked with brown signs.

The Trail

Park at the visitor center, and head to your right on the paved path to the Middle and Lower Falls. After you've checked out the falls, head up a stairway, turn right, and cross the walkway under the highway bridge. Turn left and pass the old stone visitor center. The Upper Falls are to your left.

Soon the trail meets the Superior Hiking Trail and another park trail to your right. Stay to the left along the river. The gravel and grass path is rocky and there are many roots, and you pass through the second-growth aspen and birch. Wooden bridges and walkways cross wet sections. Pass by

Gooseberry Falls

the first bridge, staying on the combined Superior Hiking Trail and Fifth Falls Trail on the east side of the Gooseberry.

Follow the sign to Fifth Falls, descending stone steps. Continue along the river for about 0.5 mile. The trail makes a moderately steep ascent as you come to Fifth Falls and another bridge over the river.

Return to the bridge and cross. At a Y-intersection, the Superior Hiking Trail bears to the right and the Fifth Falls Trail turns sharply left to continue downriver. The trail descends and passes a log shelter. About 0.5 mile from the shelter, you cross a large, flat area of rock. Pick up the trail near a

group of northern white cedars.

The trail continues along the river, with a mixed forest of birch, some pine, and shrubby underbrush. There are some ascents and descents on wide log and gravel steps and some rocky, root-covered spots.

The trail ascends steps to an overlook near an intersection. Turn left, and 0.1 mile later, stay left again on the trail nearest the river. Pass the first bridge, keeping the river to your left as you follow its oxbow curve to the Upper Falls. Continue under the MN 61 bridge. You can return to the visitor center via a path near the highway or retrace your steps past the Middle and Lower Falls.

7

Grand Portage State Park

Total distance: 2.7 miles

Approximate hiking time: 2.5 hours

Difficulty: Moderate

Vertical rise: 200 feet

Maps: USGS 7½' Pigeon Point quad, Minnesota Department of Natural Resources state park map

The "great carrying place" was part of a vast water highway that linked the commercial hub Montreal with fur-rich northwestern Canada. The Cree, Ojibwe, and Dakota tribes lived around present-day Grand Portage and traveled the chain of lakes and rivers for hundreds of years. As French explorers and missionaries went west through the Great Lakes in the late 1600s, they set up forts and fur trade posts.

Almost 100 years later, a post near the mouth of the Pigeon River became the inland headquarters of the most profitable operation, the British North West Company. At the time of the American Revolution, the post was described as the "commercial emporium" of the northwestern fur trade. Inside a cedar-picket palisade stood a great hall with business offices, warehouses, food storage and preparation buildings, and living quarters for the company's partners and clerks. From there, French-Canadian voyageurs headed west in small birchbark canoes to posts deep in the wilderness, with supplies and goods to exchange for animal pelts. Returning for an annual July rendezvous, the voyageurs and Native Americans would pass the furs to the men who had come west from Montreal in the larger canoes used on the Great Lakes. They would spend most of July celebrating and repairing canoes and other items before heading back to another season of travel and trade.

The Pigeon River connects Lake Superior with lakes and rivers stretching far into the Canadian wilderness. The name comes from the Ojibwe *omimi,* or pigeon, possibly

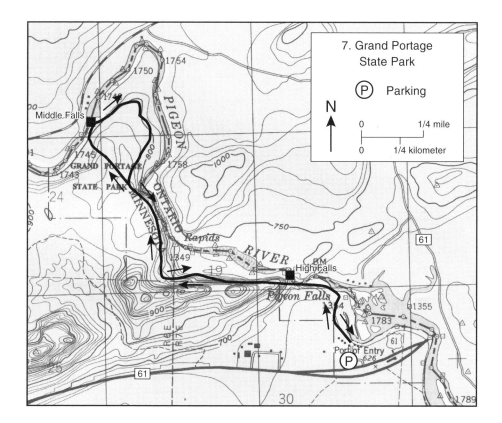

because passenger pigeons were common in Minnesota until the late 1800s. Cascades, rapids, and waterfalls make the river impassible for 20 miles upstream from the lake. That meant the voyageurs' journey started or ended with *le grand portage,* an old Ojibwe trail south of the rugged terrain surrounding the river. Voyageurs carried canoes and 90-pound packs 8.5 miles northwest from the post to Fort Charlotte, the company's smaller storage depot, where the Pigeon River was much calmer.

The Grand Portage post operated from 1784 to 1803, when the Scottish-owned North West Company abandoned it to move off American soil.

The State of Minnesota and the Grand Portage Band of Chippewa established the state park, enclosing the Middle and High falls, in 1989. The river gorge displays diabase dikes, or intrusions, into softer slates. Some of the oldest lava flows in Minnesota are found near Grand Portage.

This state park has hiking trails, a picnic area, and a visitor center with a store, but no camping facilities. The park's phone number is 218-475-2360.

How to Get There

From Duluth, travel 154 miles northeast on MN 61. The state park is 7 miles north of the town of Grand Portage and the national monument. The park entrance is on the west side of MN 61. The international border crossing is just up the road. If you miss the entrance, turn around at Canada and head back.

Grand Portage State Park

51

The Middle Falls on the Pigeon River

The Trail

The High Falls Trail begins at the parking lot as a wide asphalt path, accessible to people using wheelchairs. Signs give information about the early history of the area and logging. On our last visit, new stairs were being built leading down to the river.

Bridges, boardwalks, and steps lead to the High Falls. Head back and pick up the Middle Falls Trail, which goes off to your right at a vault toilet. It starts as crushed rock and changes over its length to packed dirt with areas of rocks, roots, overgrown vegetation, and wetness.

The trail goes through a typical mixed hardwood forest of white pine, birch, balsam fir, quaking aspen, and black and white spruce. On one visit, the ghostly white Indian pipe was growing just at the start of the Middle Falls Trail. On another trip, starflower, pink shinleaf, evening primrose, orange and yellow hawkweed, tall buttercup, yarrow, harebell, and daisy fleabane were blooming.

The first part of the trail has several moderately steep sections with rock and log steps. At about 1.2 miles a boardwalk goes over an area of lichen and exposed bedrock. You're now high enough to see Lake Superior to your left. The trail descends slightly, but you're walking above a ravine to your left. Next comes a very rocky ascent with steps and a log handrail. The trail becomes more overgrown and as it descends slightly, you can hear the sound of rushing water.

This is a wetter area with small logs cut and set in as bridges. The trail continues in moderate ups and downs with areas of roots and rocks until you come to the start of the loop. Go clockwise, to your left. You emerge into a more open area of very tall birch trees, then the trail becomes overgrown and descends toward the river, which you can see through the trees. After a steep descent, you're on the dark, erosion-resistant rock called diabase, where the water tumbles down in small rapids. Look downstream to your right to see the mist rising from the Middle Falls.

The trail continues up over the rocks to your right past a large cedar and leads to the edge of the falls, where you can sit and watch the water crash down and the mist swirl up to play over the river below.

The loop continues downriver. A short spur leads to the river's edge, where you can look back up at Middle Falls. Now the trail turns away from the river through areas of dense grasses and ferns. You pass a log bench and through thick growths of thimbleberry. A slight ascent leads you back to the start of the loop. Turn left to return to the parking area. As you look toward the river, on your left now, you'll see Canada through the trees.

Bonus Destination

Grand Portage National Monument is the reconstructed fur trade post. Just 20 years after the post was abandoned, only building foundations remained. The Grand Portage itself was described as overgrown and covered by fallen trees. The Grand Portage Band of Chippewa donated the site as a national monument in 1958. Written accounts and archeological excavations were used to reconstruct the palisade, the Great Hall with its living quarters, a lookout tower, a large warehouse, and the kitchen building. Building interiors are furnished as the post looked in 1797.

Costumed interpreters provide information about running the post, the tools used, and the people and their customs. In the kitchen building, period cooking is done with foods grown in the historic garden. Outside the palisade walls are a recreated Ojibwe village and a voyageur camp. The second week of August each year, fur trade re-enactors from across the United States and Canada gather for an annual rendezvous with music, dancing, craft demonstrations, and hands-on workshops.

The site is open daily from Memorial Day weekend through Columbus Day. The telephone number is 218-475-2202.

8

Itasca State Park

Total distance: 4.2 miles

Approximate hiking time: 2.5 hours

Difficulty: Easy

Vertical rise: Minimal

Maps: USGS 7½' Lake Itasca quad, Minnesota Department of Natural Resources

The Mississippi River starts its journey to the Gulf of Mexico in Itasca State Park. For hundreds of years, European explorers searched for the source of this great river long known to Native Americans. The river's name had 30 or more variations in maps and books published in the 1600s and 1700s. Jonathan Carver mapped the river with its current spelling in 1766. The first part of the word, *missi,* is the Ojibwe word for "great." The second part comes from the Ojibwe *sipi, sebe,* or *zibi,* meaning "river." Some historians give a fuller translation of Mississippi as "gathering in of all the waters" and "an almost endless river spread out."

The name of the lake from which the great river flows has nothing to do with Native American language, however. In 1832, explorer Henry Rowe Schoolcraft was hunting for the Mississippi's start using Native American guides. Local chief Ozawindib led him to a lake, called *Omushkos,* meaning elk. This turned out to be the Mississippi's source. Schoolcraft combined the Latin words *veritas,* meaning "truth," and *caput,* meaning "head," lopped off the first and last syllables, and came up with *Itasca,* his way of signifying "true head."

Still, the river's source was disputed—even changed and renamed by one surveyor in honor of himself—until Jacob Brower published the results of his surveys of the lake and its surrounding area in 1889. Lake Itasca was confirmed as the source, and apparently the controversy stirred up public interest in the area's geography and history. Three years later, a

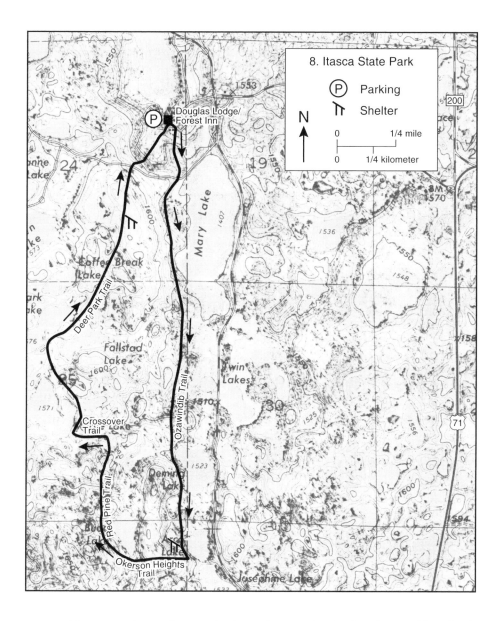

proposal to protect the area's water basin and virgin pine was presented to the Minnesota Legislature.

Today, Itasca State Park encompasses 32,000 acres of hiking and biking trails, modern and primitive campsites, historic cabins and lodges, visitor centers and gift shops, swimming beaches, and boat landings. Contact the park at 218-266-2100.

How to get there
From Park Rapids, head 20 miles north on US 71. The park has south and east entrances off US 71, and a north entrance off MN 200.

The Trail

Although the Mississippi River starts here, there isn't much of a trail at the headwaters. This hike takes you farther south in the park, away from the most heavily used areas.

Park in the Douglas Lodge/Forest Inn lot. Directly across from the Forest Inn, an interpretive center and gift shop, is an information kiosk. A brown wooden sign directs you south across a parklike area of grass to the start of the Ozawindib Trail. Signs indicate this is also the Hiking Club trail. The North Country Trail uses this path as part of its route through the park, leaving its boundary near the east entrance.

The trail crosses a bridge over Mary Creek just past the signs and continues through tall pines and a ferny understory. After 0.3 mile, you cross the paved Wilderness Drive, a circular route around a north-central chunk of the park. A chain gate and trail signs are located at the road. As you continue on, Mary Lake is visible to your left. The trail continues as a wide path varying from packed earth to mowed grass with moderate ups and downs. The surrounding forest is mixed pine and deciduous trees, like maple.

At about 0.6 mile is the intersection with the Aiton Heights Trail, going off to your right. Continue straight ahead. You see views of Mary Lake again as you near its southern shore. Here the trail becomes mossy in spots, and rocks are hidden under the grass as you follow gentle ascents and descents. Soon, you pass an open area of dead trees, and at about 1.2 miles come to another trail intersection. Continue straight ahead as you pass the Crossover Trail on your right. Just beyond this intersection, you glimpse another small lake on the left and pass a stand of old red pine.

The Okerson Heights Trail, somewhat overgrown, joins the Ozawindib at about 1.5 miles. Again, continue straight ahead.

A park shelter with a fire ring sits about 1.7 miles into this hike. The trail also intersects with the Red Pine Trail, which you follow to the right. The Ozawindib Trail continues south. The trail makes a moderately steep descent, and you pass the southern tip of a small lake. Then the Red Pine Trail curves north, to your right. The trail is fairly level here, and at about 2.5 miles Myrtle Lake comes into view. A scenic wooded island sits along the lake's northeast shore, and a campsite has been cleared and noted with a sign. This is where the Crossover Trail intersects. Beaver slides and other activity are noticeable along this part of the hike.

Harebell and purple aster were blooming along the north shore of Myrtle Lake during an August hike. Solomon's seal and columbine also were common, although past their bloom time.

About 3 miles into this hike you meet the Deer Park Trail, named for the lake straight ahead. Turn right at this intersection and walk along the lake's eastern shore. A loon was calling as it swam in Deer Park Lake, and beaver tail slaps came from across the water. Two pure white swans glided in tandem for a water touchdown.

Just north of Deer Park Lake is tiny Coffee Break Lake, with a marked campsite on your left. You pass by large pines, including one about 3 feet in diameter. An owl hooted in the woods.

At about 3.6 miles is another park shelter and fire ring where Aiton Heights Trail meets Deer Park Trail in a cleared area. Go straight ahead following the sign to Douglas Lodge. Cross Wilderness Drive again at about 3.9 miles. Here the footpath is narrower, and you enter an area of dense ferns with some

Headwaters of the Mississippi River

burned tree stumps. Just past 4 miles is the intersection with Dr. Roberts Trail, to your left. This trail is a 2-mile interpretive hike with accompanying guides available at the park's gift shop.

To return to Douglas Lodge, stay to the right. The trail becomes steeper here and has timbers set in as widely spaced steps. You meet a gravel park road that runs behind the dormitory south of Douglas Lodge. Follow this road to the right, and you'll end up back at the grassy area south of the information kiosk where this hike started.

9

Jay Cooke State Park

Total distance: 4 miles

Approximate hiking time: 2 hours

Difficulty: Moderate

Vertical rise: 200 feet

Maps: USGS 7½' Esko quad, Minnesota Department of Natural Resources state park map

At one time, banker Jay Cooke was one of the richest men in the country. Through his Philadelphia bank, he was the principal financial agent of the Union government during the Civil War. He also funded the St. Louis River Power Company in the late 1860s. The dam for the hydroelectric power plant was built just north of the park boundary, but the spectacularly rugged terrain meant the powerhouse had to be located several miles downriver. It was the 2,350 acres of land in between the two structures that Cooke's estate donated for a state park.

As it heads into the state park, the river flows through a rocky gorge and over slabs of ancient, exposed rock. Native Americans and French fur traders were used to portaging around these rapids, naming the grueling three-day trek the Grand Portage of the St. Louis. The French explorer Pierre Gaultier, Sieur de la Vérendrye, apparently named the river to honor the king of France during the Crusades.

The park's geology is called the Thomson Formation, which got its start in the vast sea that covered Minnesota 2 billion years ago. Mud, sand, and gravel that settled on the sea floor were compacted over millions of years into shale and sandstone. Ripple marks can be seen on rocks in the park. Heat and pressure continued to compress the rock into slate and a dark-colored sandstone called graywacke. Millions more years of pressure folded the slates at sharp angles.

Later, molten rock flowed up through cracks in the rock. Geologists call these

Coniferous Forests

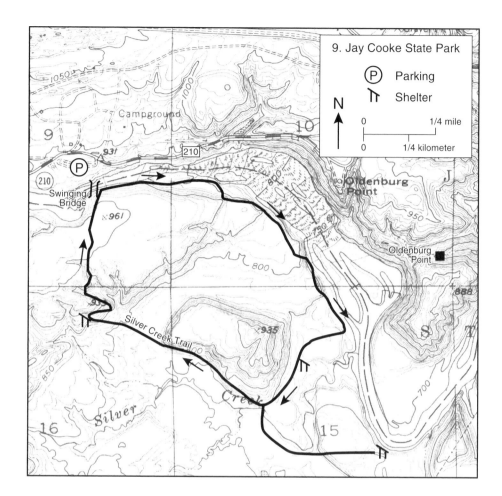

intruded rock formations dikes. These ancient formations were exposed after the glacial meltwater of the St. Louis River's ancestor cut through sediments and into the underlying rock.

Near the center of the park, exposed slate abruptly ends and the river smoothes out, flowing through banks of red clay left by an ancient glacial lake that flooded the river valley.

Because of the rugged, rocky terrain, much of the area along the river was spared from farming. The park features several rustic stone and log buildings that are listed on the National Register of Historic Places. A large suspension bridge with rock bases spans the river. Men living in a Civilian Conservation Corps camp during the 1930s built the structures.

The park has an 80-site campground with restrooms and showers. Twenty-one of the sites have electricity. One camper cabin with a screen porch, heat, electricity, and nearby flush toilets and showers is available for rent. Two group camps, three backpacking campsites, two picnic areas, and a trailer dump station are located in the park. To contact the park, call 218-384-4610.

Slanted graywacke along the St. Louis River

How to Get There

From Duluth, head south approximately 15 miles on I-35 to the Carleton exit. Turn east on MN 210, passing through the village of Thomson, for about 7 miles.

The Trail

Park at the River Inn Visitor Center, one of the park's beautiful stone buildings. Just east of the park is an asphalt walkway that leads south to the swinging bridge. Cross the bridge, stopping to take in the view of the tilted bedrock and tea-colored water churning over tumultuous rapids up- and downstream. You can feel the bridge move under your feet.

At the other end of the bridge, the trail splits. You can walk out on the rocks, closer to the river, if you turn right. Check out the rock formation now or when you return to the same spot at the end of this hike.

At the end of the bridge, take the trail to the left closest to the water. Ascend a few

steps and follow the wide dirt path that goes above the river. Head down some steps to a river view. Be careful, there's no railing here.

Second-growth birch, maple, aspen, ash and some northern white cedar grow in this area. Here, the river continues to demonstrate why this "Grand Portage" was necessary. The trail narrows and descends slightly into a wetter area with grasses and ferns growing waist-high over the trail. You can literally walk right into the river, but just before this point the trail angles to your right. At a T-intersection, turn left. The trail stays near the river as it curves south and separates into braids.

A park shelter sits on the red clay bank above Silver Creek, offering a view of Oldenburg Point to the east. The trail now follows Silver Creek to your left.

About 1.5 miles from the start of this hike, you come to an intersection marked 37. Bear left and shortly cross a bridge over Silver Creek. The trail follows the creek to the left. The next intersection is marked 38. To the left is the High Landing backpacking campsite. Straight ahead is a shelter. Now you're at the end of Oldenburg Point, and the river makes a sharp turn north. As it continues toward the park's eastern boundary, the St. Louis River flows through a wide gorge of red clay.

After taking in the view, retrace your steps back to marker 38, then along and over the creek to marker 37. Turn left onto the Silver Creek Trail and cross a bridge. This is a low, wet woodland, and the trail can be wet. Beavers also are active in this area.

Continue along the bluff to your right. Ascent to another shelter offers a resting spot. According to park staff, this hillside is where yellow lady's slipper can be seen blooming in spring.

The trail takes a sharp left turn just past the shelter, then shortly meets an intersection with the Ridge Trail, marked 53. Turn right, and meet intersection 31 in 0.1 mile. Continue straight ahead to intersection 32. Five trails converge in this area. Take the next trail left to the river, and you end up back at the tilted graywacke just south of the bridge. Cross the bridge to the visitor center.

10

Judge C. R. Magney State Park

Total distance: 2.5 miles

Approximate hiking time: 1.5 hours

Difficulty: Lots of steps make it challenging in spots

Vertical rise: 240 feet

Maps: USGS 7½' Marr Island quad, Minnesota Department of Natural Resources state park map

The cascade at Judge C. R. Magney State Park is unique among North Shore waterfalls. It was formed from the same molten lava that erupted 1.2 billion years ago, then hardened up to 21,000 feet deep. As the lava flows thickened, a great basin sank to the east of the rift. Glaciers scoured the earth's surface, and streams and rivers eroded valleys and canyons as they made their way to the sunken area that became Lake Superior over thousands of years. Most of the lava hardened into dark basalt, but rhyolite also is found. The Brule River rhyolite flow is thought to be as much as 3,500 feet thick.

In this park, rhyolite juts up and divides the Brule River in two. On the eastern side, water crashes into a pool, then continues its rocky way to Lake Superior. Water rushing around the other side of the rock plunges into a huge pothole named the Devil's Kettle and disappears—at least until it too, presumably, joins the lake.

The park is the site of a government camp built to provide work and lodging for transient men during the Depression. The men raised food, built fire trails, cut trees, completed public service projects, and built a riverside tourist park. Concrete foundations from camp buildings are visible in the park's campground and picnic areas.

A state park called Bois Brule State Park, named after the river, was established in 1957. Ojibwe called the river *wissakode zibi,* or "half-burnt-wood river." The name translated to the French *brûlé,* meaning burnt and pronounced *broo·LAY.* The river

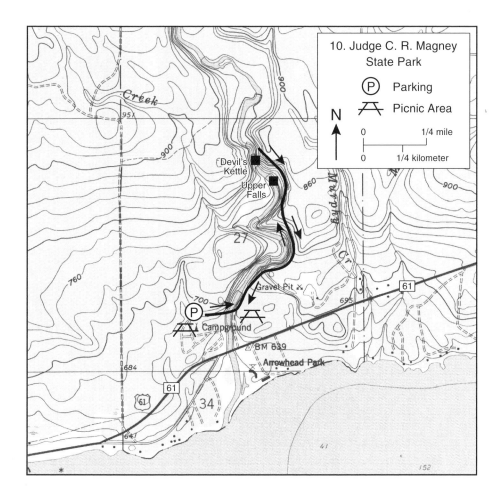

begins in the Boundary Waters Canoe Area Wilderness and flows undeveloped to Lake Superior.

The name changed in 1963 to honor Judge Clarence R. Magney, a mayor of Duluth, a Minnesota Supreme Court Justice, and avid trout fisherman who had died the year before. A nature advocate, Magney helped establish 11 of the North Shore's state parks and waysides. A memorial to Magney, located along this hike, gives his philosophy: "Our state parks are everyone's country estate."

The park has 9 miles of hiking trails, 5 miles of cross-country skiing trails, 27 semi- modern campsites, and a picnic area. All the facilities are at the eastern, lakeside end of the park, leaving most of the land in this long, narrow park wild and undeveloped. Elevations vary greatly throughout the park, and a large variety of habitats can be found. Areas of pine are interspersed among birch and aspen. Black spruce grow in swampy lowlands. White spruce can be found on higher ground, and white cedar appear to grow out of solid rock.

The diverse vegetation supports abundant wildlife. Pine martens, fishers, red foxes, otters, and coyotes live in undeveloped areas.

The Devil's Kettle in Judge C. R. Magney State Park

Moose, white-tailed deer, black bears, and timber wolves are seen in all areas. Ruffed grouse, nuthatches, woodpeckers, hawks, and a variety of warblers are seen in the park. The phone number is 218-387-3039.

How to Get There

From Grand Marais, drive 14 miles northeast on MN 61. The park entrance is directly off the road, on the west side.

The Trail

Park in the lot next to the picnic area. The trail starts at a large sign designating the Superior Hiking Trail, Devil's Kettle Trail, National Recreation Trail, and Hiking Club Trail. You will cross a board bridge over a small stream. To your left is a large rock, which displays the Magney memorial. Cross a bridge with green metal railings over the Brule River. On the other side of the river is a picnic area with a toilet.

Turn left onto the Devil's Kettle Trail. A large number of steps make this hike somewhat challenging. Here, the wide gravel trail ascends. Old white pines grow along the trail and across the river. You also pass areas where the white pine is being restored. These areas have been enclosed to keep deer from eating the seedlings.

Forest understory is typical boreal vegetation of club moss, bluebead lily, and lots of bunchberry. Early spring wildflowers include marsh marigold, wood anemone, and violet. Summer gives way to wild rose, thimbleberry, twin-flower, and cow parsnip. When we hiked in mid-August, asters and fireweed were blooming.

The trail heads up 23 steps and continues along the river gorge. About 0.4 mile into this hike, you pass a bench. Continue heading upriver.

Just 0.5 mile later you come to a well-built staircase with about 200 steps that descends to a boardwalk and a view of the Upper Falls. Another 21 steps take you down to the river's edge. Look for a sign that reads "Devil's Kettle 700 ft." It's up another 57 steps to the overlook.

The Superior Hiking Trail continues upriver past the Devil's Kettle. We retraced our steps down the Brule to the parking area.

11

Lake Walk, Superior Hiking Trail

Total distance: 1.6 miles

Approximate hiking time: 1 hour

Difficulty: Easy

Vertical rise: None

Maps: USGS 7½' Marr Island quad, Minnesota Department of Natural Resources

This is the only section of the Superior Hiking Trail right on the lake. Beaches with flat rocks or cobbles are common along Lake Superior. Waves and erosion break off pieces of the ancient volcanic rock, which are further shaped by water and sand. Waves continually carry sand, gravel, and rocks to and from the shoreline. Rounded rocks roll back into the lake with the waves, leaving flat rocks to pile up on shore.

The rocks in this area are mostly 2- to 4-inch cobbles of red felsite. Some gray basalt and granite are mixed in. The shoreline juts out in several points and knobs. However, waves constantly are rearranging the shore. Our family spends a week on Madeline Island, one of Lake Superior's Apostle Islands, each summer. Each morning, the beach outside our rented house is different. The spot where we put the lawn chairs today may be underwater tomorrow.

The older beaches of Lake Superior's glacial ancestors are farther inland. At the start and end of this hike, you walk through old beach ridges that are wet and boggy. Birch, spruce, and alder grow here, along with wildflowers like butter-and-eggs and jewelweed.

This hike starts just past the village of Colville, which is named for Colonel William Colvill. For some reason, an *e* was added to his name. Born in Forestville, NY, Colvill moved to Red Wing in 1854 and started the *Red Wing Sentinel* newspaper. He fought with the First Minnesota Heavy Artillery, and was at Gettysburg when the regiment lost

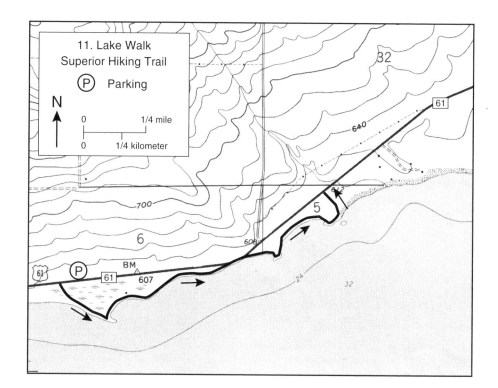

a majority of its soldiers trying to plug a hole in the skirmish line. He was a Minnesota legislator and state attorney general, then homesteaded a claim on Lake Superior's shore in his later years.

How to Get There

From Grand Marais, head northeast on MN 61 for 12 miles. Just past the Kadunce River Wayside, at highway milepost 120.2, look for a Superior Hiking Trail sign. The parking area holds only a few cars, so it's easy to miss.

The Trail

This is a one-way hike, so you might have someone drop you off and pick you up on the other end. Although this isn't a long hike, and it stays level, walking on the cobbles isn't easy. Because the rocks slide around, the beach isn't a firm walking surface. It's harder than you would expect.

Follow the Superior Hiking Trail to the lake as you pass through birch and alder trees and shrubby underbrush. At the beach, turn left. The shore angles out to a point with a small offshore island. This was an early morning hike, and the pastel light of the sky on the lake and rocks was beautiful. The biting flies, however, were horrible. You never can predict when flies will be bothersome, so if it's cool enough, wear long pants.

Walk along the beach, or stop to skip some of the flat stones, for about 1 mile. The highway comes close to the lake here. The trail curves right as it follows a knob of shoreline that creates a small cove.

You can see the shoreline ahead of you curve out in another knob. Cross an area of

A small islet juts into Lake Superior

boulders and ancient lava flow with the shallow, water-filled depressions common along the North Shore. Now you come to an offshore island and another that could be reached by a small gravel bar. This made a lovely spot to sit and watch the lake. Back on shore, look for a Superior Hiking Trail sign next to an opening in the vegetation. This sign reads EAST END OF LAKE WALK, JUDGE MAGNEY PARKING 5.2 MI. It's a short walk through overgrown grasses and wildflowers and across boards over a wet area to the road.

Coniferous Forests

12

Mille Lacs Kathio State Park

Total distance: 3.2 miles

*Approximate hiking time: 1 hour,
40 minutes*

Difficulty: Moderate with difficult spots

Vertical rise: 50 feet

*Maps: USGS 7½' Vineland and Onamia
NW quads, Minnesota Department of
Natural Resources state park map*

This park contains one of the most archae-ologically important sites in Minnesota and is designated a National Historic Landmark. People have lived in the area for more than 9,000 years. The earliest site contains evidence of copper toolmaking. The Dakota called the large lake on the park's north-eastern border *Mde Wakan*–sacred water. Several communities of the Mdewakantan branch of the Dakota still live in Minnesota.

The lake and its surrounding forest provided a variety of food, including wild rice, fish, and water birds for native people. Archaeological digs along the park's Ogechie Lake have revealed the remains of houses, pottery, arrowheads, and stone and bone tools. Burial mounds, most closely associated with the Dakota, also are located along the lake. Archaeologists estimate that up to 25,000 mounds may have existed in Minnesota, but erosion, agriculture, road construction, and burrowing animals have destroyed most of them.

As Europeans pushed further west in North America, they displaced Native peoples. French explorers first traveled through the region in 1679 and 1680. It's their name for the lakes area–*Mille Lacs* or "thousand lakes"–that survives today. The origin of the Kathio part of the name is less straightforward. Daniel Greysolon, Sieur du Luht, referred to a Dakota village as *Izatys* in 1679. This might have been a variation of the Issati or Isanti division of Dakota, according to one state historian. Greysolon's handwriting later was misread, with a "K" in place of the "Iz" and "hio" in place of the

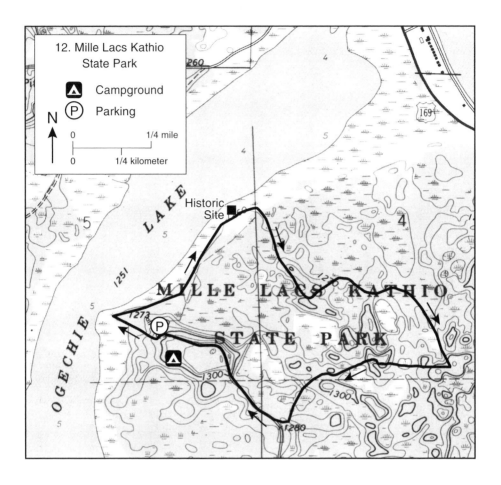

12. Mille Lacs Kathio
State Park

🔺 Campground

Ⓟ Parking

N

0   1/4 mile

0   1/4 kilometer

"ys." The erroneous name was repeated in numerous maps and reports and became attached to the park.

Dakota domination of this area ended when the Ojibwe migrated into the northern Great Lakes region from the St. Lawrence River area farther east. Ojibwe oral history tells of a massive single battle that drove the Dakota from the area and established Ojibwe dominance. Archaeologists haven't found evidence of massive battles, but think that small skirmishes must have occurred. The Ojibwe had the advantage of European firearms. Eventually, the Dakota moved south and west. Today the Mille Lacs Band of Ojibwe lives in the area and operates a profitable casino.

As happened in much of the state, loggers came to work the area in the 1850s. By the turn of the 20th century, the vast growths of white and red pine were gone. Second-growth aspen, birch, maple, oak, and other northern hardwoods make up the forest of today's 10,000-acre park.

The terrain is part of a large terminal glacial moraine. An advance of the Superior Lobe of the Wisconsin glacier stalled and left piles of sediment large enough to dam the flow of meltwater and create the immense Mille Lacs Lake.

Coniferous Forests

Facilities are concentrated on the west side of this large park. There are two campgrounds, and 20 sites with electricity are available. The park has 19 semimodern and 26 rustic camping spaces, along with three hike-in spots. This park also has five camper cabins with screen porches, heat, electricity, and nearby flush toilets and showers. A horseback campground and picnic area with a swimming pond are available. Boat launches are located along the Rum River and Shakopee Lake. Contact the park at 320-532-3523.

How to Get There

Located about 80 miles north of Minneapolis–St. Paul, the main park entrance is 1 mile off US 169. Turn south on Mille Lacs County 26. At the park information office, turn right and drive about 3.2 miles to the Kathio Landmark Trail parking area, just past the Ogechie campground.

The Trail

From the west side of the parking area, head toward the flat, grassy area along Ogechie Lake. The name comes from an Ojibwe word for an intestinal worm and refers to the lake's skinny shape.

Find the gravel path marked with interpretive signs. This also is a Hiking Club trail. Pass a sign with information about a prehistoric Dakota village that was located on a peninsula to your left. Pass a path leading back to the parking area. Ancient burial mounds—low, rounded masses of earth—are located in this area. Turn right to read the three remaining interpretive signs, then backtrack to the Hiking Club trail.

In about 0.5 mile the trail curves left and descends to a mowed area near the lake.

This is the site of one prehistoric village where 30 to 40 people lived. Follow the Hiking Club sign and ascend a terrace above a pioneer homestead. The trail ascends slightly, curves around an open meadow with a small marshy area to the left, and continues with a few more slight ascents and descents.

At the next intersection, marker 16, turn left, following the Hiking Club route. For about 0.4 mile the trail ascends slightly to a ridge, then heads down into a ravine, and back up. As we hiked, a deer ran across the trail. This section has short, somewhat steep hills passing small wetlands. Go up a somewhat steep incline.

At a Y-intersection, marker 15, bear right onto a trail marked with a zigzag "most difficult" sign. To your left is a wetland, and the trail passes lots of moss-covered stumps and rocks. Make a sharp right turn at the next intersection of several trails, marker 14, again following the Hiking Club route. Horseback riders also use this section of trail. Watch out for rocks and roots in the packed dirt trail. In about 0.3 mile you pass through an area of ponds and marshes. There is evidence of beaver activity, and we watched as a beaver slid silently through the water, leaving its V-shaped wake. Pass a hiking/horse trail, marker 25, that comes in from your left. We met two more deer here. Bear right at intersection 24.

At the next intersection, marked 23 and with another "most difficult" sign, turn right. After about 0.1 mile, turn left at marker 19. The narrow trail climbs two steep hills before you reach the park road. Turn right and walk about 0.3 mile back to the parking area, passing by Ogechie campgrounds on your left.

13

Oberg Mountain

Total distance: 2.4 miles

Approximate hiking time: 1.5 hours

Difficulty: Moderate

Vertical rise: 315 feet

Maps: USGS 7½' Honeymoon Mountain quad, Superior National Forest map

Oberg Mountain is one of the more distinctive heights among the volcanic formations along the North Shore. It's part of the lava flows that oozed up from cracks as this part of North America split apart about 1.2 billion years ago. Geologists think the lava originated from the center of Lake Superior's present location. As the underlying magma flowed out, the weight of the layers caused the area to sink. Later lava flows ran down toward the sag.

Even after millions of year of erosion, the northwestern sides of these mounds remain steeper, giving the ridge the serrated appearance that spawned the name Sawtooth Mountains. To early settlers, the jagged, somewhat regular outline resembled the teeth of a giant saw.

Oberg Mountain is among the intrusions of a dark rock called diabase.

Like much of northern Minnesota, the area around Oberg Mountain was logged off in the late 1800s. In his 1963 state history book, Theodore Blegen writes that a poet once said "America is West," but a forest historian said that "when explorers landed, America was trees." In northern Minnesota, those trees were white pine. Treaties in which Native Americans gave up pinelands in East Central Minnesota in 1837 cleared the way for wholesale logging. In 1859, Governor Alexander Ramsey reported the export of 33 million feet of sawed lumber. By 1876, lumber production reached 193 million feet! Duluth became a major logging center after the Civil War.

The peak production year was 1905, and the decline was swift. Some lumber compa-

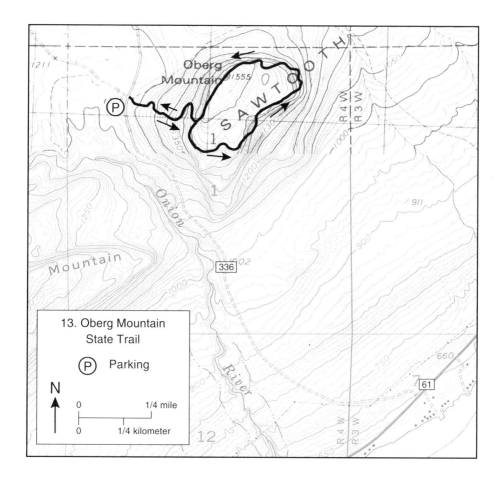

13. Oberg Mountain
State Trail

Ⓟ Parking

N

0 — 1/4 mile
0 — 1/4 kilometer

nies switched to making paper and began cutting spruce, aspen, birch, and cedar.

Historians caution that the ruthlessness of Minnesota's lumber industry has to be viewed in the context of its time. People regarded the forests as endless. In 1855, a newspaper claimed the state's pinelands "may never be exhausted," according to Blegen. "Forests were swept away by a generation that exploited the resources of nature as it found them and met needs as fast as forest, men, machines, and ingenuity permitted."

It wasn't until the 1930s that the state's planning board pointed out that little virgin timber remained and much of the second growth was poor. The condition of Minnesota's forests made clear "the necessity of sober middle age," the board said. Efforts at conservation and reforestation began to take hold.

The results of those efforts can be seen as you hike around Oberg Mountain. The six overlooks provide views of the second-growth maple, birch, and pine forest. Maples love the warmer ridgetops, and hiking this trail in fall offers much color.

The Oberg Mountain Trail is within the Superior National Forest's Tofte Ranger District. The ranger office telephone number is 218-663-8060.

Lake Superior view

How to Get There

From Tofte, which is approximately 80 miles north of Duluth, head about 5 miles northeast on MN 61. Turn west on the Onion River Road, which is the gravel Forest Road 336. Drive 2.2 miles to a large parking lot, marked with a Superior Hiking Trail and cross-country skiing sign, on the south side of the road.

The Trail

The Oberg Mountain Trail starts across the road from the parking area. A trail to Leveaux Mountain leaves the south side of the parking lot.

Ascend some stairs. A sign gives information about the Youth Conservation Corps' construction of the trail. Continue about 0.2 mile to the intersection with the Superior Hiking Trail, which heads left to Moose Mountain.

Turn right and begin a moderate ascent, then start walking up the moderately steep switchbacks. The forest floor is somewhat open with vegetation typical of the boreal forest. Bloodroot, common strawberry, bluebead lily, bunchberry, starflower, columbine, aster, and goldenrod bloom at various times.

The loop around Oberg Mountain starts about 0.5 mile from the beginning of this hike. At the first overlook, the trees give way to rock. Below you is a valley with a sweep of trees as far as the eye can see to Leveaux Mountain. A second overlook of Leveaux Mountain comes shortly.

In about 0.4 mile is another overlook with a picnic table seemingly created for a giant. The huge logs give the table odd proportions, but it's a great place to sit and enjoy the view. Follow the trail about 0.3 mile to the sixth overlook at the edge of a rocky, steep cliff. Continue to your left for the last overlook, which is a view of Oberg Lake set among the carpet of trees to the west. The sun was beginning to set as we reached this point, and the deepening colors made the view even more spectacular.

Continue to the start of the loop and turn right, to the Superior Hiking Trail. Descend the switchbacks to the intersection with the Superior Hiking Trail, which you've passed before. Retrace your steps to the parking area.

14

Savanna Portage State Park

Total distance: 5.4 miles

Approximate hiking time: 3 hours

Difficulty: Easy

Vertical rise: 50 feet

Maps: USGS 7½' Balsam and Little Prairie Lake quads, Minnesota Department of Natural Resources state park map

The Savanna Portage linked Lake Superior via the St. Louis River with the inland upper Mississippi River. The name comes from the small open areas of grass and shrubs along the Savanna River in terrain that is generally wooded. The portage trail was an old Native American path that explorers and French fur traders began using when they came to the area in the mid-1700s. A son of the famed explorer and trader LaVérendrye was one of the earliest voyageurs to trek through the marshy area.

Later fur traders came up the St. Louis River, portaging around especially rocky rapids, then poled canoes as far as possible up the shallow, mucky, debris-clogged East Savanna River. "A perfect quagmire," according to a member of an expedition led by Henry Schoolcraft, who found the source of the Mississippi River in 1832.

The 6-mile portage started on poles laid lengthwise through a tamarack swamp. Voyageurs usually carried two packs weighing about 90 pounds each. Portages were broken into sections with rest stops, literally called pauses.

The portage route gradually rises along sandy ridges, then ends in a marsh at the West Savanna River. The trip took about five days, but the trek got easier after that. Big Sandy Lake, leading to the upper Mississippi River, was only 3 miles from the portage's western end.

Mosquitoes and flies, annoying to hikers who can use modern repellents, must have been merciless to voyageurs. One Savanna

Coniferous Forests

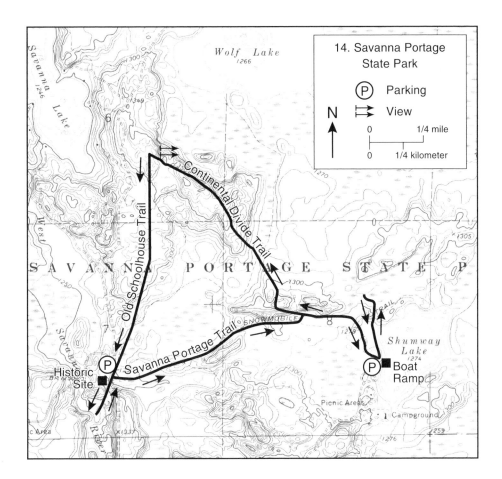

State Park ranger just shook his head in disbelief when answering questions about the portage, its marshy environment, and voyageurs' tenacity.

The park's interesting history is matched by its unique geological feature—a ridge where to the east, water drains to the Atlantic Ocean, and to the west, water ends up in the Gulf of Mexico via the Mississippi. The ridges, rolling hills, and sandy soil are glacial leftovers.

Park habitat includes marshes and bogs. The large bogs are old glacial lakes, which have changed through a process called bog succession. Over thousands of years, veg- etation growth and accumulating sediment reduce the amount of open water. Sometimes, floating mats of sphagnum moss support trees and other vegetation.

Savanna State Park's bogs support some of nature's most beautiful wildflowers. We saw burgundy and lime-green pitcher plant, deep pink stemless lady slipper, and deep purple wild iris during an early July hike. At other times, northern white violet, marsh marigold, bog rosemary, and early buttercup bloom. More than 100 kinds of wildflowers and blooming shrubs grow in the wooded areas and along the roads of this park.

Boardwalk through a marsh on the historic Savanna Portage

Because of the different habitats, a wide variety of wildlife lives here. Bears, deer, skunks, moose, wolves, coyotes, and lemmings are seen.

Park facilities include a campground with 63 semimodern sites, 17 of which have electricity, restrooms, and showers. There are also seven backpack campsites, one canoe campsite, and a primitive group camp. A rental cabin, with heat, is available. A fishing pier and boat ramp are located on Lake Shumway. Loon Lake has a swimming area, boat ramp, and picnic grounds. Boats and canoes can be rented. Contact the park by calling 218-426-3271.

How to Get There
From McGregor, head northeast on US 65 for 17 miles. Turn northeast onto Aitkin County 14 and drive 10 miles to the park entrance.

The Trail
Turn right at the park information office to the campground and Lake Shumway boat ramp. Park at the boat ramp.

The Bog Boardwalk, a 0.3 mile spur off the Lake Shumway Trail, is worth taking. At the boat ramp, turn left along the lake shore. Wild iris, or blue flag, was blooming here. Meet the bog trail in about 0.3 mile. As the name implies, the trail descends a glacial esker, a thin ridge, onto a wooden boardwalk that ends at a bog lake. The moss and wildflowers grow so artfully that a landscape architect would have a tough time coming up with a more beautiful setting.

Return to the parking area, and turn right. Find the Continental Divide Trail, marked with a blue Hiking Club sign, just past the pit toilets. The trail is a wide, mowed path. Rusted machinery sits in the trees to your

Coniferous Forests

left. Pass a trail that comes in from the left and continue straight ahead on the Hiking Club trail.

The trail curves left, then descends to a five-way intersection the park staff calls "Spaghetti Junction." Continue straight ahead on the Continental Divide Trail, passing the historic portage path and a trail to Wolf Lake. The trail continues along a ridgetop. In about 1 mile you come to a campsite with a pit toilet on your left.

The Continental Divide lookout platform is on the right. The large wooden deck with railings overlooks Wolf Lake and a surrounding tamarack lowland, also called a forest bog. Signs explain the different watersheds on either side of the divide.

Just past the lookout is a four-way intersection with the Old Schoolhouse Trail. Turn left. This section was very wet. The mosquitoes and flies almost brought Gwen to tears but deepened her appreciation of voyageurs. The trail continues with gentle ascents and descents and meets the park road in about 1.6 miles.

Turn left and walk on the road for about 100 paces to the Savanna Portage Trail parking area on your right. This is a very large mowed area with a pit toilet. Walk across the open area to a historical marker and sign. The trail descends to the West Savanna River, where the voyageurs got back into their canoes and headed to Big Sandy Lake and the upper Mississippi.

Retrace your steps to the parking area and head back down the road a few steps. The historic trail starts across the large marsh on your left. Modern-day visitors have the luxury of a wooden boardwalk, but Native Americans and voyageurs had to slog through the mud, water, and aquatic plants. A sign halfway across tells of the Dakota name *mushkigonigumi* for "marsh portage."

The trail enters aspen at the east end of the marsh. Pass a trail to your right that returns to Lake Shumway. Follow the Portage Trail sign and bear left. Ascend to a ridgetop, where you'll see interpretive signs along the narrow footpath. The next trail intersections can be confusing, but keep following the PORTAGE TRAIL signs. Turn right at the next intersection. There is a marsh on the right side of the trail. Next is an area of red pine, then a left turn at another Portage Trail sign.

A slight ascent brings you back to the five-way intersection. From here the historic trail gets rougher as it continues 5 miles east to East Savanna River. Walk a ways down this narrow footpath to continue reliving the voyageur experience. When you're ready, retrace your steps to the five-way trail crossing, and turn left following the Lake Shumway and Hiking Club signs. Return to the parking area.

15

Split Rock River, Superior Hiking Trail

Total distance: 5 miles

Approximate hiking time: 3.5 hours

Difficulty: Moderate with steep sections

Vertical rise: 220 feet

Maps: USGS 7½' Split Rock Point quad, Minnesota Department of Natural Resources state park map, and Superior Hiking Trail map

The Superior Hiking Trail Association calls this one of the trail's premier day hikes. It combines many of the North Shore's scenic features into one loop. Start with a tea-colored river tumbling over cliffs and rock ledges. Add dramatic rock formations sculpted by glaciers. Continue with sand-carved potholes. Throw in birch, pine, and cedar. End with a sweeping view of Lake Superior, and you've got this hike.

The rock in this river gorge is rhyolite, a fine-grained, reddish igneous rock with much the same chemical composition as granite. This rock came from the same volcanic upheaval that formed the North Shore 1.2 billon years ago. The rhyolite formed vertical cracks as it cooled. About 10 miles north, Palisade Head and Shovel Point in Tettegouche State Park are high rhyolite sills that show the same vertical, columnlike cracks.

These fractures made it easier for glacial meltwater to erode a gorge, forming steep cliffs and ledges over thousands of years. Erosion continues, and the loose chips along the trail result from frost action.

All this rock cleavage probably gave the river its name. Stories point to the split rocks of the gorge and, specifically, a large rock formation that has split down the middle into two tall pillars, which you pass on this hike.

A logging company operated at the mouth of the river from 1899 through 1906. A spur railroad hauled cut trees out of the forest surrounding the river. The last section of this hike follows the Merrill Logging Trail.

Coniferous Forests

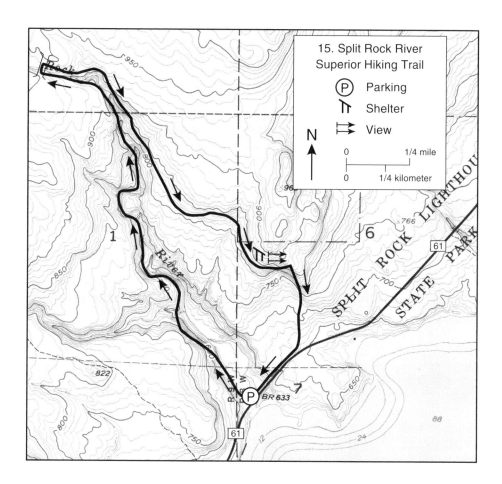

At the lake, logs were lashed into giant rafts and hauled by tugboat to Duluth. These lesser waterways were an important part of the lumber industry system, and Duluth enlarged its docks because of the lumber trade and grew into a city. Rafting logs was "in itself a specialized business and one of high importance," according to Theodore Blegen's 1963 state history book. Rafting companies were formed, operating as independent enterprises.

How to Get There
From Duluth, drive 33 miles northeast on MN 61 to Castle Danger. Continue north and pass Gooseberry Falls State Park. Look for highway marker 43 and go about 0.3 mile to a wayside rest on the west side (your left) of the roadway.

The Trail
Find the trail at the large signboard at the parking lot's southwest corner. Although five vehicles were parked in the lot, we didn't meet anyone else on the trail.

The trail ascends through birch forest with the river valley to your right, then shortly you descend a series of wide steps. At about 0.5 mile is an intersection with a Superior Hiking Trail sign. Gooseberry Falls

Potholes along the Split Rock River

State Park is to your left, southwest, 4.3 miles. Turn right on the Split Rock River Loop. Descend more than 50 timber steps to a NO CAMPING sign and a bridge over the west branch of the river with a small waterfall. There is a hiking club box with a notebook, where hikers have recorded their impressions. Most seemed to be enjoying themselves.

Climb about 30 steps, then descend gently as the trail narrows. A steeper ascent up rock steps brings you to another small waterfall. There is a bench, and spur trails lead to the river for a closer look.

The trail continues and boardwalks cross gullies in the rocky terrain. Soon you come to rapids below another waterfall. The trail climbs, with some steps, to the falls. Cross a board bridge, then rock steps up a moderately steep incline. The trail heads directly toward the river, onto bare rock. Climb the very steep rock cliff to your left.

At about 1.5 miles you leave Split Rock Lighthouse State Park. The narrow footpath descends to the river again. Watch your step in this area of loose rock with steep ascents and descents. Next you come to the split rock pillars rising from the rock next to the river.

Pass the Southwest Split Rock River campsite, and continue to the site of the old bridge, which washed out in 1997. You can climb down to the rocks here and see small potholes formed by abrasive sand and pebbles swirling round and round. Head back to the trail and walk about 0.25 mile upstream to the new bridge. The Northwest Split Rock River campsite sits atop a small hill in a stand of cedar.

The new bridge was built by trail association volunteers, who started the process by shimmying over a wire strung across the river. After admiring the builders' handiwork as you cross the bridge, turn right to head down the river's east side. A sign tells you a park shelter is 1.5 miles down the trail.

About 0.3 mile from the bridge is the Northeast Split Rock River campsite. The trail rises above the river, and you cross a log bridge. The Southeast Split Rock River campsite is across from the stone pillars. This is a favorite camping place, but the latrine is located up a steep grade.

The next section of trail continues up and down over moderate hills and crosses a rocky area on a high cliff. The ascent becomes gentler as you enter an area of birch and aspen with shrubs, ferns, and grasses. As you approach the log park shelter, the wide vista of Lake Superior lies ahead. You can see Split Rock Lighthouse off to your left.

The trail descends the hill and comes to an intersection. The Superior Hiking Trail continues toward Beaver Bay 10.8 miles northeast. Stay on the right-hand trail as it makes a moderate rocky descent to an intersection with the Merrill Logging Trail. Turn right on the wide mowed path marked with a CAUTION STEEP HILL AHEAD sign.

Reach MN 61 through a field of tall grass. Gwen almost stepped on a rotting deer carcass here. Walk on the west edge of the road, to the right of the guardrail. Here the river flattens and moves at a slower pace through a wide valley. The wayside parking area is straight ahead.

16

Split Rock Lighthouse State Park

Total distance: 2 miles

Approximate hiking time: 1.5 hours

Difficulty: Moderate with steep sections

Vertical rise: 240 feet

Maps: USGS 7½' Split Rock Point quad, Minnesota Department of Natural Resources state park map

Split Rock Lighthouse is one of Minnesota's best-known landmarks. In the early 1900s, Lake Superior was busy with ships hauling iron ore. After storms wrecked 30 ships in 1905, the United States Lighthouse Service decided to build the lighthouse, fog signal, and keepers' dwellings. Over 300 tons of building material had to be lifted from boats up the cliff face. Perched on a 130-foot-high cliff, the octagonal brick lighthouse was accessible only from the water when it began operation in 1910. A derrick was used to load and unload supplies from boats. Later, bulk quantities of coal, gasoline, and kerosene needed to run the lighthouse equipment were hauled up the cliff via a tramway.

When MN 61 was completed in 1924, Split Rock Lighthouse became an instant tourist destination. Modern navigation technology spelled the end of the lighthouse's working life in 1969. It became a historic site two years later. The Minnesota Historical Society operates the lighthouse, restored to look as it did in the early 1920s, and gives tours daily May 15 through October 15. Costumed interpreters depict lightkeepers and their families, and describe the famous lake storms. The rest of the year, only the history center is open Fridays, Saturdays, and Sundays.

The rocky North Shore of Lake Superior was formed by volcanic eruptions about 1.2 billion years ago. Layer upon layer of lava flowed over the area, sometimes dragging up huge chunks of underlying rock. Differences in erodibility account for the variations in rock formations along the North Shore. The

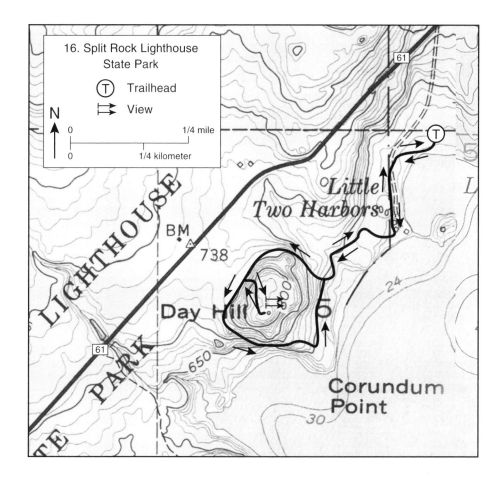

cliff on which the lighthouse sits is a massive sill, or intrusion, of erosion-resistant diabase topped by a light-green anorthosite.

Before the lighthouse was built, a small group of fishermen lived in a small village next to a cove at the park's southern end. These Norwegian fishermen hauled in herring at Little Two Harbors from the turn of the 20th century until the 1920s. The group never exceeded 12 men, who left when the land's owner asked them to pay rent.

About the same time, a company was mining what it thought was corundum, crushed and used as an abrasive, south of the fishing village. Turned out the rock was

the much softer anorthosite, which wasn't as good for the intended use, and mining stopped. You can see the remains of mine buildings and equipment.

As in much of Northern Minnesota, loggers cut down the original red and white pine. Fires then burned whatever trees were left. Today birch dominates the park area, and land management includes erecting fences to keep deer from eating pine and cedar seedlings. You see these deer "exclosures" along the trails.

This is a popular park. Facilities include a campground where people park, then use lightweight carts to haul their gear to one of

The famous Split Rock Lighthouse

20 secluded sites. Showers and restrooms are located in the campground. Kayak and backpack campsites also are available, and the park has a picnic area. The telephone number is 218-226-6377.

How to Get There
Drive 45 miles northeast of Duluth on MN 61. The park's entrance is well marked.

The Trail
Park at the trail center, south of the lighthouse and history center. Head toward the lake and turn right onto the Little Two Harbors Trail. Pass the picnic area along the lake to your left. The small cove is a nice place to stop and skip the flat, smooth rocks that make up many Lake Superior beaches. Pass spur trails to the cart-in campsites and the site of the old fishing village.

Turn left toward the Day Hill Trail loop after you pass the campground registration building, on your right. The loop starts after about 0.1 mile. We went right and started ascending the base of the hill. After about 0.4 mile, the hiking trail meets the paved Gitchi Gami State Trail as part of a four-way intersection. Turn left to begin the ascent of Day Hill. The steep trail rises about 100 feet in little more than 0.1 mile. The summit offers spectacular views of the lighthouse and the lake spreading to the horizon below it. A large stone fireplace also sits at the top of the hill. A story tells of landowner Frank Day, who started to build a house where he would live with the woman he had asked to marry him. She changed her mind, and the fireplace is all that remains.

Head down the hill when you're ready, and turn left onto the paved trail for about 0.1 mile. Turn left at the next intersection marked with a CAUTION LONG STEEP HILL AHEAD sign. The steep trail is a wide grassy path with some rocks. At the bottom of the hill is a grassy area with a trail that leads to Corundum Point to your right. Turn left.

You come to a large number of wooden steps and platforms. Climb up—we counted more than 100 steps—along a massive rock wall on your left. The rock is a welcome cool spot during a hike that raises your body temperature. At the start of the Day Hill loop, turn right and retrace your steps back to the trail center.

17

St. Croix State Forest

Total distance: 9.5 miles

Approximate hiking time: 4 hours, 45 minutes

Difficulty: Moderate

Vertical rise: 100 feet

Maps: USGS 7½' Danbury West quad, Minnesota Department of Natural Resources state forest map

Minnesota has 57 state forests, and the Department of Natural Resources manages more than 4 million acres of forest land. This one is located in Pine County, named for its original extensive red and white pine forests, which lumbermen almost completely cut down in the early part of the 20th century. Today, St. Croix State Forest is a mix of old and young maple, basswood, ash, aspen, oak, red and white pine, and tamarack.

The forest borders the St. Croix River, but hiking trails also follow the Tamarack River, named for the tree. This is the only coniferous tree that drops its needles—after they turn gold—every fall. Tamaracks, also known as eastern larch, like swamps and bogs.

How to Get There

From Hinckley, head east on MN 48 for 23 miles. Turn north on Pine County 173 for about 5 miles, then head east, a right turn, onto Tamarack Forest Road. Follow the road, passing the intersection with the horse camp road, about 6 miles to the Boulder Campground on Rock Lake.

The Trail

This hike can be wet in spots, and you also have to cross the Tamarack River where there is no bridge. Toting a pair of lightweight sandals will mean you can keep your feet dry the rest of the hike.

Park near the boat launch. Walk south of the launch and look for campsite 18. Follow a rutted path in the grass to the left. The trail goes up and down several ravines, and a bridge crosses a marshy area. Lots of small

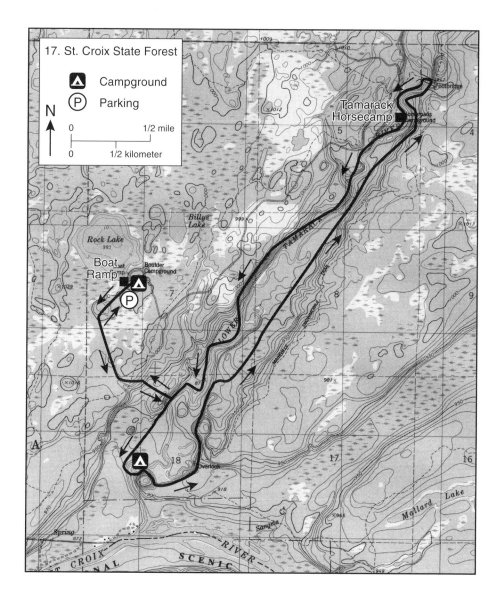

trees and shrubs overgrow the trail. At a Y-intersection, bear left and keep walking through young maples.

After just over a mile, you come to a four-way intersection. Continue straight ahead. At the next intersection, turn right to start the river loop. The trail ascends in switchbacks to the top of a ridge, then descends to the river. This area can be muddy. The trail rejoins the river at an oxbow curve. This is where you cross, in water that usually is several feet deep. A state forest employee advised that the water can get higher and faster if there's been a lot of rain.

On the other side of the river, you again climb to a high ridge via switchbacks. Turn

---

St. Croix State Forest

The Tamarack River

left, toward the Pine Point campsite, at the next intersection. This high knob with pines has a pit toilet, picnic tables, and fire pit. Pass a trail to your right, and continue along the river to an intersection with St. Croix State Snowmobile and ATV Trail. Stay to your left toward the Tamarack horse camp.

The trail goes to the riverbottom floodplain. About 1 mile past Pine Point campsite, the trail makes a sharp right away from the river. Continue through the mixed maple, basswood, aspen, and pine forest for another mile before the trail climbs out of the river valley, over a small stream.

Pass campsite 3. The trail comes back to the river's edge. Pass campsite 2. The trail follows the river's curves to the bridge at the horse camp. Cross and turn left, again following the river's curves past the horse camp to your right. About 0.9 mile past the

bridge is a trail that angles right and crosses the forest road. Continue straight along the riverbank, with some ascents and descents, for the next 1.25 miles. Pass by another trail that comes in from your right.

The trails along the next section can be confusing. At the next intersection, a trail to the right makes a hairpin curve and ascends a ridge through a series of switchbacks. However, stay left along the river, following it to a picturesque bend. The sandy trail is overgrown with grasses and ferns here.

The trail makes a sharp right and climbs up from the river valley. The trees here are young with some dense shrubby underbrush. Next you come to an intersection where you turn left to campsite 5. You should be back at the intersection where you started the river loop. Turn right and head back to Rock Lake and Boulder Campground.

Coniferous Forests

18

St. Croix State Park

Total distance: 6.5 miles

Approximate hiking time: 3 hours, 15 minutes

Difficulty: Easy

Vertical rise: Minimal

Maps: USGS 7½' Lake Clayton quad, Minnesota Department of Natural Resources state park map

Native Americans, then French, British, and American fur traders used the St. Croix River as a main trade route for hundreds of years. The name of the river as St. Croix, or Holy Cross, shows up on maps and proclamations by 1689. Apparently, a cross was set up at the river's mouth, marking the grave of a French trader or voyageur.

As in much of northern Minnesota, St. Croix State Park's virgin red and white pine forests were cut down during the logging years. Camps were built along the river to float logs to sawmills downstream.

When logging died out, farmers moved onto the cleared land, but the poor soil made it tough to make a living. During the Depression of the 1930s, the federal government bought poor farmland to convert to recreational use. The National Park Service, the CCC, and the Works Progress Administration began building roads, campgrounds, and other structures on about 18,000 acres in 1935. The stone buildings and structures still are in use and are listed on the National Register of Historic Sites. Actually, the National Park Service has designated the entire park a National Historic Landmark.

The St. Croix River valley was a major drainage channel when the last glaciers melted from Minnesota about 10,000 years ago. The glaciers left more than 31 types of soil on top of the bedrock within the park. One area along the river was named Yellow Banks for its deposits of yellow clay.

While the St. Croix forms part of the park's eastern boundary, many other streams and creeks flow through the park—making for

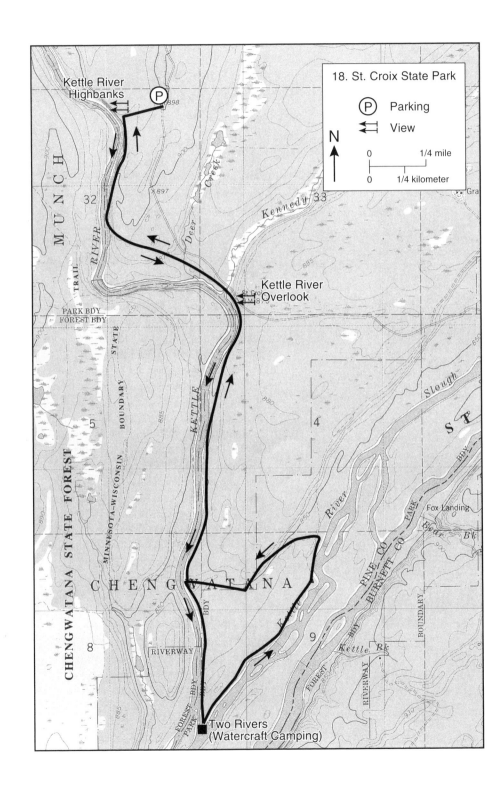

Kettle River
Highbanks

(P) 898

18. St. Croix State Park

(P) Parking

◄═ View

N

0   1/4 mile

0   1/4 kilometer

Gra

M   U   N   C   H

32

897

RIVER

TRAIL

Deer   Creek

Kennedy   33

885

Kettle River
Overlook

St. Cro
48

PARK BDY
FOREST BDY

STATE

5

BOUNDARY

MINNESOTA-WISCONSIN

KETTLE

885

880

4

880

Slough

S   T

CHENGWATANA   STATE   FOREST

River

PINE CO

BDY

BURNETT CO.

PARK

Fox Landing

Bear   Bk

890

C   H   E   N   G   W   A   T   A   N   A

850

9

Kettle   Bk.

BOUNDARY

8

RIVERWAY

Kettle

FOREST   BDY

RIVERWAY

885

FOREST BDY
PARK BDY

Two Rivers
(Watercraft Camping)

The St. Croix and Kettle rivers meet

lots of canoe access sites. On the park's west side is the Kettle River. Along its banks, glacial meltwater left the basalt and sandstone bedrock exposed, as you'll see where this hike starts. The two rivers meet at a point on this hike.

St. Croix is Minnesota's largest state park, at 33,000 acres, with more than 100 miles of multi-use trails, 215 campground sites, five camping cabins, and several hike-in campsites. Even so, we met only two other vehicles on our way back from this hike, near the main road into the park.

Given its size, the park supports many diverse habitats. Black spruce and tamarack bogs, sugar maple and basswood forests, jack pine barrens, and meadows have grown up where the native pine once stood.

How to Get There

From Hinckley, go 15 miles east on MN 48. The park's entrance is marked with a large stonework sign. Park headquarters, in one of the historic stone buildings, is 5 miles south of the entrance.

The Trail

At the intersection just south of park headquarters, head west, toward the beach. The road soon turns to gravel. Drive about 8 miles west until you get to the Kettle River Highbanks parking area. (You'll notice the park's size as you drive along at the 20-miles-per-hour speed limit.) A short trail leads about 0.25 mile to the river bank. Here you see the exposed bedrock.

Turn south and head downstream. The trail follows the river for about 0.5 mile, then turns left to the park road. Walk on the road about 0.4 mile until you see the trail marker on your right, just past the Kettle River Overlook parking area. The wide grassy trail makes its way back to the river. Again, head downstream to your left. The packed-dirt trail is narrow but mostly level, and for the next mile you pass through areas of mixed second-growth sugar maple, basswood, birch, and aspen. You also cross several planks over wet areas. It rained the day of our hike, so some of the overgrown planks—hard to see anyway—were slippery.

Pines along the Kettle River

Several lovely stands of tall pines line the riverbank, one just before reaching an intersection about 2.5 miles from start of this hike. The trail to your left cuts across to the St. Croix River. Continue straight ahead along the Kettle.

Three miles into this hike the Kettle and St. Croix Rivers meet. Standing at the Two Rivers campsite looking south, you can see how the rivers differ. The narrower Kettle moves more briskly over small rapids, while the wider, slower St. Croix divides into braids and meanders around small wooded islands. The campsite, which offers a picnic table, fire ring, and latrine, was empty the day we hiked.

The trail now turns up the other side of this small peninsula to follow the St. Croix. It also gets overgrown, with shoulder-high vegetation, and is hard to see at times. Stay toward the river to pick up the narrow footpath. Short boardwalks on this side of the trail cover deeper gullies, so watch your step. For the next mile, you'll push through areas of small trees, shrubs, and shoulder-high aquatic grasses. You pass several large patches of beautiful maidenhair ferns with their arcs of delicate leaflets.

A clearing marks another canoe campsite, again with picnic table, fire ring, and latrine. Several large pines give this site its Pine Ridge name. Just beyond the campsite is the crossover trail left to the Kettle River. You can continue straight on a wide grass road through maple, oak, and some pine for 1.1 miles until you meet the park road at Gate 25. Turn left and follow the gravel road for another 1.75 miles back to your car.

However, we enjoy the more scenic riverside walking and turned left on the crossover trail. The wide grass trail follows a gentle up-and-down course through the same mixed hardwood and coniferous forest for 0.7 mile before intersecting with the Kettle River. Here we turned north, to our right, and retraced our steps back to the Kettle River Highbanks parking area.

Coniferous Forests

19

Sturgeon River Trail

Total distance: 2.5 miles

Approximate hiking time: 1.5 hours

Difficulty: Easy

Vertical rise: Minimal

Maps: USGS 7½' Dewey Lake NW quad, USDA Forest Service map

The Sturgeon River starts in the lake of the same name on the western boundary of St. Louis County. One of several Sturgeon Lakes in Minnesota, this northern one is named for the rock sturgeon. This fish can grow to 6 feet in length and weigh up to 100 pounds. At the turn of the twentieth century, sturgeon fishing was a chief occupation on lakes farther north, along the Canadian border.

The Sturgeon River flows southeast into the Mesabi Iron Range. The name comes from several transformations of the Ojibwe *missabé wachu,* meaning "big man hills," or *missabe wudjiu,* meaning "giant mountain." This meaning seems to conjure up visions of great heights. However, the state's iron ranges are level belts of land with a few high hills and ridges.

The iron formed from sediment deposited in a Middle Precambrian sea about 2 billion years ago. It contained rounded pellets and oolites, which have concentric rings indicating they were formed by rolling in waves or currents of shallow water. This ancient geological period was "the age of iron," write two University of Minnesota-Duluth geology professors in their 1982 book *Minnesota's Geology.* "Never before and never since has there been such a period of deposition of iron materials." The world's other major iron formations are the same age.

The state's first geologist reported iron in the area in 1866 but dismissed the outcrops, saying "To hell with iron. It's gold we're after." The first Mesabi Range iron ore was shipped out 26 years later, after the three Merritt brothers and two of their nephews discovered a site near Mountain Iron.

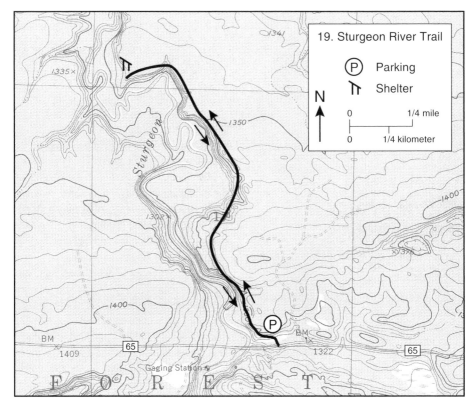

P Parking

Ⴑ Shelter

N

0   1/4 mile

0   1/4 kilometer

In this range, as in the older Vermilion area to the north, a slight ridge merges with level land on the southwest but rises roughly a few hundred feet at its eastern end. Along its foothills are the ore deposits, usually of the soft variety, lying in broad stretches, more horizontal than in the Vermilion Range. The iron formation in the Mesabi Range dipped down slightly, with few exposures at the earth's surface. However, the overlying soil was easy to remove, and the high-grade ore itself was soft. This meant it could be mined in large open pits. Hundreds of these open-pit mines were worked on the Mesabi Range.

High-grade ore began running out in the 1950s and 1960s. University of Minnesota scientists had developed a process to mine lower-grade taconite and concentrate it into pellets, and taconite production came to

dominate the industry. It was the area's primary export by the 1980s, but has since declined.

As in most of Minnesota, glaciers sculpted the landforms long after the ancient sea had disappeared. The area's low, rolling hills with steep valleys are moraines: accumulations of boulders, stones, and other glacial debris. At nearby McCarthy Beach State Park, where the river starts in Sturgeon Lake, the namesake beach is a glacial moraine.

When settlers reached the area, gigantic red and white pines covered the hills. Logging started in the area about 1895. Wood from area sawmills built the booming mining town of Hibbing, about 20 miles south of where this hike starts.

The Superior National Forest, in which this trail lies, was set aside as a public forest

Coniferous Forests

Tall pines on the Sturgeon River Trail

reservation in 1909. The intention was to preserve the area for forestry uses. Today, the Superior National Forest encompasses much of northeastern Minnesota north of Duluth to the Canadian border.

How to Get There

From Chisholm, drive about 12 miles north on MN 73. Turn west on St. Louis County 65, a gravel road. After about 1.2 miles you come to a large parking area on the north side, your right.

The Trail

This hike is only a small sample of the 20-mile Sturgeon River Trail system, which follows the river north and south of the county road. Trail parking areas also are located along MN 73.

At the CR 65 parking area, head for the map and holders for paper maps at the northwest corner of the cleared spot. Bring your own map in case the holder is empty.

Head to your left up a short, grass-covered hill. A deer skeleton lay hidden in the tall grass. The trailhead can be hard to find. Go through a small wooded area, then into another clearing. A sign marks the beginning of the trail as you reenter the woods.

The trail goes along a ridge with a steep decline to your left. The river is down below, but you can't see it from here. Continue as the trail makes several gentle descents, then slowly ascends. The forest is a mix of typical second-growth birch, aspen, and some pine. However, you pass through one spot of gorgeous tall red pine. The pine needles are thick on the trail, making for soft steps and a quintessential North Woods smell. Bunchberry, orange hawk-weed, and wild rose were blooming during an early July hike.

The trail curves right, away from the river and through a low, wet area. The trail is overgrown here with tall grasses and waist-high ferns. There were several small spots of standing water and mud. Small blue-diamond signs mark the trail, but they're sometimes hidden in the brush.

The river, which you still can't see, takes a sharp turn east and heads closer to the trail about 1.3 miles into this hike. But you can hear the water off and on as the river makes sharp oxbow curves below the ridge to your left.

The trail continues along the ridgeline through areas of saplings and taller trees. The trail curves left, following the river but still above it. Among some larger pines is a shelter with a fire ring. A trail leads down the riverbank. It's a very steep climb down to the soft mud of the riverbank, where a mass of arrowhead was growing. The Sturgeon River flows slower, around a bend here.

Climb up the steep bank. The trail continues northeast more than 3 miles to a parking area along MN 73, then down along the west side of the river. Because of a time crunch, we rested at the shelter, then retraced our steps back to the parking area.

Bonus Destination

Ironworld Discovery Center in Chisholm preserves the region's mining and immigration history with interactive visitor displays, mine views, and library and archival facilities. Ironworld's museum features a permanent exhibit about Iron Range history, a standard-gauge railroad experience aboard a 1928 vintage trolley, a living history site with preserved buildings, and a daily program that provides visitor interpretation. It is open during the summer and early fall. An admission fee is charged. The Iron Range Research Center, open all year, identifies and collects records that preserve the history of the Iron Range. Ironworld's toll-free telephone number is 1-800-372-6437.

20

Superior National Forest, Bass Lake Trail

Total distance: 5.6 miles

Approximate hiking time: 3.5 hours

Difficulty: Moderate

Vertical rise: 100 feet

Maps: USGS 7½' Ely quad, Superior National Forest map

President Teddy Roosevelt proclaimed on Feb. 13, 1909 that large sections of three northern Minnesota counties—Cook, Lake, and St. Louis—be set aside as a public forest reservation. The intention was to preserve the area for forestry uses. T. R. was worried that the country was using up natural resources without any thought to management and the future.

In 2004, the federal government unveiled long-range plans that would allow slightly more logging in nonwilderness areas of the National Forests. Neither the environmentalists nor the timber industry is happy with the plan.

Superior National Forest boasts more than 2,000 lakes and rivers, along with countless ponds, bogs, and marshes. Most of the hundreds of lake basins near the Canadian border sit in bedrock basins scraped out by glaciers, which exaggerated natural fault lines to create irregular shapes.

Native Americans used the waterways for centuries. Ancient pictographs can be seen on the rock cliffs along several lakes, including Hegman Lake, 6 miles north of Ely. Trappers and French voyageurs moved into the area in the 1800s, then came miners and loggers.

South of Bass Lake, extremely high-grade iron ore was mined near Ely. This ore was deeper in the earth's surface and had to be excavated through shafts. The underground mine shafts had to be supported with timber, so local logging operations and sawmills developed.

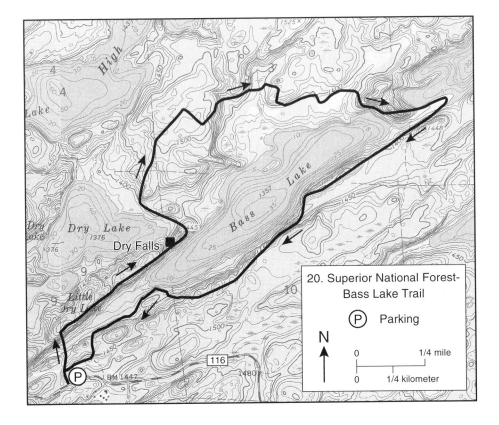

20. Superior National Forest-
Bass Lake Trail

(P) Parking

N

| 0 | 1/4 mile |
| 0 | 1/4 kilometer |

Bass Lake's history is tied directly to one of these logging operations. In the early 1900s, loggers built a wooden trough on top of a glacial gravel ridge between Bass and Low Lakes. It was easier to float logs through the trough, or sluiceway, on their way to a local sawmill. When the logging operation stopped, the water-filled trough was left untended. Seeping water weakened the glacial ridge, which broke apart with a great roar in 1925. Bass Lake dropped by 55 feet, leaving exposed lake bed and three smaller lakes, one with a waterfall.

According to the Forest Service, the old lakebed is recreating ecological events that were commonplace when glaciers melted here 10,000 years ago. Plant succession from mosses to shrubs to young maple and aspen can be seen.

Just south of Bass Lake lies a long, narrow area of low land between rock ridges, which is part of the Vermilion Fault System.

How to Get There

From Ely, head north on US 169 to St. Louis County 88 and turn west. Turn north on St. Louis County 116, called the Echo Trail, to the trailhead parking area on the east side of the road.

The Trail

The trail starts at a sign with a map of hiking trails and Bass Lake's history and a vault toilet. Cross a boardwalk, and you come to a

Coniferous Forests

Bass Lake

Y-intersection. Follow the wordless brown and white metal hiking sign to your right. At the next intersection is a brown sign marking trail options. Turn left as indicated by the arrow to Dry Falls. Cross a bridge with one railing over a small stream.

The trail ascends steeply, with one switchback, as you climb to the top of a ridge overlooking the forest and former lake to your right. You walk through pine and see aspen below. There are several spots where you can walk to the edge of the ridge to see the old lakebed and a meandering stream that flows through it. About 1 mile into this hike is a steep descent to a rocky bluff overlooking Bass Lake. The trail continues a steep rocky descent to Dry Falls. After climbing down large rock outcrops, you cross a bridge over the stream running through rocky ridges and cascading into Bass Lake.

Immediately after the bridge, the trail ascends steeply and you come to an un-marked intersection. To the left is a short spur trail along the rocks with a view of Dry Lake, and a lovely peninsula, down to its shore. To continue on the main trail, go right. Shortly, you come to a four-way intersection. The trail to your right leads to lakeside campsites. To your left is a trail to Dry Lake. Continue straight ahead.

Pass another campsite sign on your left. At the next intersection, go straight ahead on the Bass Lake Trail.

Next comes a rocky ascent before the trail levels out. For about the next 0.5 mile the trail continues over rock outcrops marked with rockpiles and more artistic cairns. About 2 miles from the start of this hike is a view of the north half of Bass Lake.

The trail descends into the old lakebed, a flat, sandy area where grasses and young aspen and maple are growing. Pearly ever-lasting, asters, and goldenrod were blooming in early September.

The trail continues over wet areas where boardwalks and coarse rock pathways have been built. Pass a campsite with a picnic table and fire ring.

As you near the glacial ridge, the coarse sand turns to pebbles, then small rocks. At one point, the view in front of you is a ridge of small rocks slanting toward the lake. The trail cuts a horizontal curve through the mass of natural cobblestones. The ridge rises to your left, a mostly barren hillside. To your right is the muddy old lakebed.

The trail continues across the sandbar between Bass and Low Lakes. Two groups of canoe paddlers had set up camp here. It's hard to pick up the trail here, so go to the channel between the lakes and walk to your right. Look for a short boardwalk. Cross it, then go over a larger bridge, and you'll see the hiking sign marking the trail to your right.

The trail ascends through birch, balsam, and red pine. The lake is to your right now, just visible through the trees. After about 1 mile you come to another overlook, a rock cliff with jack pine along its edge. Now the trail descends through some extremely rocky areas. We hiked in a light mist, so the rocks and roots were very slippery. Pass by tall rock outcrops to your left and an area of leaning, moss-covered cedars that mark the old shoreline. This area of trail has several short boardwalks over wet areas.

Soon you can hear Dry Falls from across the lake. The trail descends to the lake's southwestern shore, where a flat sandy area is a canoe access point. Continue on the trail to your left, following the hiking signs. Ascend two small flights of log steps before you end up back at the large trail sign. Continue straight ahead to the parking area.

21

Superior National Forest, George Washington Memorial Pines Trail

Total distance: 2.3 miles

Approximate hiking time: 1 hour, 15 minutes

Difficulty: Easy

Vertical rise: Minimal

Maps: USGS 7½' Grand Marais quad, Superior National Forest map

Much of the forest along the Gunflint Trail—one of the few major roads in this part of Minnesota—burned in a 1927 fire. Five years later, Grand Marais Boy Scout Troop No. 67 decided to plant 32 acres with 14,570 Norway, or red, pine and 7,500 white pine seedlings. Replanting has been done several times since, and members of the Youth Conservation Corps pruned some of the older trees in 1975.

What is now known as the Gunflint Trail was a footpath for Native Americans and European explorers. The name comes from Gunflint Lake, where early explorers found the flintlike red chert or jasper, used to ignite gunpowder and start fires. In more modern history—1870—the path was widened from Grand Marais to the eastern end of Rove Lake, where a trading post was located. By 1893, the primitive dirt road was extended to Gunflint Lake and Cross River. When automobiles came into wider use, the former path was turned into a gravel road.

Today, the Gunflint Trail is Cook County 12, a 57-mile paved road that is maintained year round. The eastern end is in Grand Marais and it travels northwest through the Boundary Waters Canoe Area Wilderness to just below the Canadian border. The Gunflint Trail ends at Seagull Lake, where there is a campground. Gas is available at several locations, but there are no actual gas stations. There are many resorts off the Gunflint Trail, and about 200 people live in this remote area year round.

Some of the 70-year-old pines

How to Get There

From Grand Marais, turn northwest on the Gunflint Trail, Cook County 12. Drive 8 miles to a four-car parking area on the west side of the road.

The Trail

This is a cross-country skiing trail that is not groomed. It gets enough use to make the trail visible, although it is overgrown in spots and goes through a wet area next to Elbow Creek.

The trail starts to the left of a wooden information kiosk. Go straight ahead to a one-way sign indicating the direction for cross-country skiers. Turn right. The trail is wide, with knee-high grasses and some rocks. Here birch trees and cedar grow on the edge of the pine plantings, which mostly are to your left.

After about 0.6 mile you come to a faint Y-intersection; bear left. The trail makes a sharp left curve and is overgrown and rocky. You can hear Elbow Creek to your right as you walk through waist-high ferns and shorter horsetails.

The trail follows the creek, which can be heard but not seen through the trees. After about 0.5 mile, the trail and creek curve right. Along this section of trail are two wet, marshy spots. Logs have been set into the muck, and it's possible to cross without getting your feet wet if you're careful. At one point, the shrubby river vegetation thins enough for you to push down to Elbow Creek, a small, fairly quick-running stream.

Back on the trail, you cross a wide wooden bridge. Every once in a while a hole shows up in the trail, so watch your step. The trail ascends very slightly above the creek, which you can see through the trees.

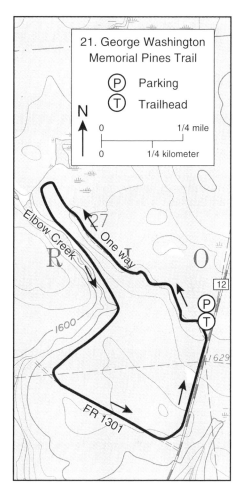

Cross another wide wooden bridge over a wet area.

The trail turns left to follow an old forest road. This is the best section of the memorial pines. The sound of the wind rushing through their tops and the smell on a warm July day made us grateful for the Boys Scouts' hard work. After about 0.5 mile on the old forest road, you meet the Gunflint Trail. Walk alongside the road back to the parking area.

22

Superior National Forest and Boundary Waters Canoe Area Wilderness, Eagle Mountain Trail

Total distance: 7 miles

Approximate hiking time: 4 hours

Difficulty: Moderate and steep to summit

Vertical rise: 550 feet

Maps: USGS 7½' Eagle Mountain quad, USDA Forest Service map

Eagle Mountain is the highest point in Minnesota, although it wasn't always so recognized. Ulysses S. Grant II, the president's son, and state geologist Newton Winchell thought that a peak 6 miles north was higher and measured that spot at 2,230 feet in the 1890s. It wasn't until 1961 that a US Interior Department aerial photography survey found Eagle Mountain to be 2,301 feet high.

The mountaintop is part of the geologic Duluth complex, mostly coarse-grained, dark-colored igneous rocks. The slow-cooling magma formed hard crystals that resisted erosion by glaciers. This bedrock begins to show through the vegetation as you near the peak, which is marked with a brass plaque.

Most of the trail is within the Boundary Waters Canoe Area Wilderness, so a day permit is required for hiking. The nearest National Forest ranger station is in Grand Marais. The phone number is 218-387-1750.

How to Get There

From Grand Marais, the way to Eagle Mountain is well marked with brown road signs. Head north on Cook County 12, known as the Gunflint Trail, for about 3.5 miles to Cook County 8. Head west about 6 miles to Cook County 27, which is a gravel road to your right. Continue about 5 miles, past the USDA Forest Service's Two Island Lake campground. Turn left at Forest Road 170, where the green street sign reads "The Grade." Continue for another 5 miles to the well-marked Eagle Mountain Trail parking lot on the north side of the road.

Coniferous Forests

The Trail

At the trailhead, fill out a day permit at the kiosk. A vault toilet is located here. This is a rugged trail, and you might have to remind yourself to stop and look around. The first part of the trail ascends and descends through black spruce, birch, and fir. The walking surface varies from packed dirt to pine needle cover to jagged rock. Just before entry to the Boundary Waters, after about 1 mile, you cross a boardwalk over a marsh. From here to Whale Lake, boardwalks cross boggy areas and a creek. On a perfect blue-sky day in July a yellow pond lily was blooming, and arrowhead stuck up among the aquatic plants.

You reach Whale Lake after about 2.2 miles. A trail to a campsite goes off to your left and is marked with a sign. Just past this intersection a large area of bindweed was blooming. The trail continues along Whale Lake's cedar and spruce shoreline for about 0.5 mile. It is very rugged here, with 3- to 4-foot rocks and many tree roots. At the northwest corner of the lake, about 3 miles into the hike, is a sign marking a trail to Brule Lake 6 miles to the east and another campsite on Whale Lake's north shore.

Follow the trail to your left for the ascent of Eagle Mountain. The trail rises steeply, including a spot where you climb through boulders tilted at a 45-degree angle to your left and loose rock and boulders to your right. As you near the top of Eagle Mountain, areas of bare rock, lichen, and moss are exposed as the jack pines thin. The first vista of the surrounding forest to your left shows how high you've climbed. The trail continues over exposed bedrock, and you come to another sweeping view. If you want to reach the plaque marking the summit, don't stop here. Look to your right and head over the exposed bedrock toward rock cairns marking the trail. The plaque sits in some brush

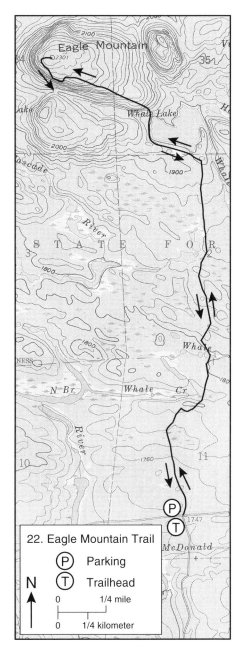

22. Eagle Mountain Trail

Ⓟ Parking
N Ⓣ Trailhead

0   1/4 mile

0   1/4 kilometer

Near Eagle Mountain's summit

that blocks the view down the mountain. Head back down to the open area to take in the dramatic view of the Misquah Hills to the north and numerous lakes joined by rivers to the west and south.

Even though seven other people were at various points along the trail, no one else shared the breeze at the very top of Minnesota. What goes up must come down, and given this trail's ruggedness, it isn't a carefree descent. Gwen's tumble on the exposed roots along the west side of Whale Lake, with a skinned knee and bruised hip, attests to that.

23

Superior National Forest and Boundary Waters Canoe Area Wilderness, North Arm Trails

Total distance: 6.1 miles

Approximate hiking time: 3 hours, 45 minutes

Difficulty: Easy

Vertical rise: Minimal

Maps: USGS 7½' Shagawa Lake quad, USDA Forest Service map

The Boundary Waters make up the northern third of Superior National Forest. Approximately 1.3 million acres, running nearly 150 miles along the Canadian border, are designated "areas where the earth and its community of life are untrammeled by people." Because the area that became the Boundary Waters was first set aside in 1926, its pristine qualities have been maintained. Congress passed the Wilderness Act of 1964 to ensure "an enduring resource of wilderness," and the Boundary Waters was included.

Geologically, the Boundary Waters sits on the lower portion of the Canadian Shield, North America's nucleus. Layer upon layer of molten rock flowed up through cracks in the earth's surface and hardened. New lava pushed and tilted older flows. Millions of years later, glaciers scraped and gouged the bedrock. Glacial meltwater created rocky gorges and filled depressions.

Today this geologic history is seen in the 1,175 lakes larger than 10 acres and hundreds of miles of rivers and streams. Twenty percent of the Boundary Waters' surface area *is* water. While most people canoe through the Boundary Waters, hikers aren't left out. There are 16 hiking trails, some of which start outside the area in the Superior National Forest. Cross-country skiing trails also can be hiked.

Such a large area obviously shelters lots of wildlife. A large, stable gray wolf population lives in the Boundary Waters, along with red foxes, lynx, fisher, pine martens, mink,

Coniferous Forests

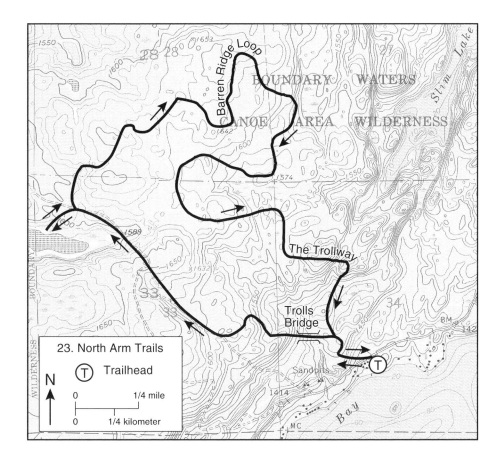

23. North Arm Trails

N

T Trailhead

0   1/4 mile

0   1/4 kilometer

otter, weasels, black bears, moose, beavers, white-tailed deer, and porcupines. As Gwen stood reading a map at the side of a gravel road, a red fox came trotting out of the brush. It stopped and looked at her for several seconds, then bounced across the road.

The American Bird Conservancy has named the Boundary Waters one of 100 Globally Important Bird Areas. The area provides habitat for many species of migrating birds. Year-round residents include pileated woodpeckers, ruffed and spruce grouse, and great horned owls.

A huge storm on July 4, 1999 has altered the Boundary Waters. Ninety-mile-per-hour winds uprooted and broke off trees in a 4- to 12-mile wide, 30-mile swath along the Canadian border. Brush has grown up where the forest canopy is gone. You can see some areas of downed trees on this hike, but it's not in the hardest-hit area.

Day trips into the Boundary Waters require only self-issued permits at trailheads. The section at the front of this book covering the Boundary Waters Canoe Area Wilderness has more information about hiking and camping in this unique area. The Kawishiwi district office of the Superior National Forest is in Ely. The phone number is 218-365-7600.

The Sentinels

How to Get There

From Ely, head northeast on US 169, then take a left onto St. Louis County 88. The road curves so that you're heading west. Turn north, a right, onto St. Louis County 116, called the Echo Trail, for 2 miles. Drive 9.4 miles to St. Louis County 644, or North Arm Road. Head west, a left turn, for 3.5 miles. The North Arm Trail parking area is on the north side of the road.

The Trail

These trails primarily are used for cross-country skiing, but they're open to hikers. All the intersections have mapboards, but at several rocky spots the trails themselves weren't evident. We were surprised to find ourselves in a place other than where we expected, but just chose another trail to continue our hike.

Stop at the information kiosk and fill out a day permit for hiking in the Boundary Waters

Canoe Area Wilderness. Continue past the kiosk to a three-way intersection of the Moose Horn Loops to your right and Slim Lake straight ahead. Turn left onto the North Star and Trollsway trails. The trail ascends slightly, and you pass a trail to the left. The rocky trail passes a bench and curves left. Here you come to the Sentinels, two white pines more than 300 years old, whose roots cross over the trail.

Cross a boardwalk. At a Y-intersection with a bench, head left. About 0.5 mile from the start of this hike, you cross what the Forest Service has named the Troll's Bridge. It's just a wooden bridge over a rocky ravine.

At the next intersection, go left onto the Hug-a-Tree trail section, which is rocky and root-covered. In about 0.4 mile is the intersection with the Coxey Pond Trail. This is an old two-track road, so hiking is easy here. Turn right and walk through young maple and red pine and mature birch. Continue straight ahead as you pass the intersection of Thor's Trail to your right and Ole Lake Trail to your left.

Soon you come to a section of downed trees in standing water, which was partially covering the road when we hiked. A large beaver dam sits in the middle of the area.

At the next intersection, take the spur trail to your left to Repose Lake. This is a narrow footpath with roots on a slight decline. Pitcher plant and Labrador tea grow along the boggy shoreline. Retrace your steps back to the intersection and continue straight across onto the North Star Run. Here the footpath passes through knee-high ferns and taller red pine. This is where you enter the Boundary Waters. Walk through areas of tall pine and overturned trees with rocks held in the roots. Typical boreal forest floor plants like bluebead lily and bunchberry held their colorful berries when we hiked in September.

After about 0.6 mile on this trail section, you come to the intersection with the Lost Lake Trail to your left. Continue straight ahead and start crossing large areas of rock outcroppings. Follow the numerous rock cairns along this part of the trail.

At the next intersection, turn left onto the Barren Ridge Trail. For the next mile you walk over rock outcrops swathed with caribou moss and lichen. The patchwork of muted pastels from the pink granite and gray-green moss are especially lovely. Soon you come to a large rock outcrop.

This is where we missed a mapboard intersection. We went straight ahead over the large outcrop, following a blue diamond marking. This put us on the Troll's Way, which meets up with Toivo's Trail after about 0.6 mile. Pass by this trail, continuing straight. In another 0.4 mile, you meet the other end of Thor's Trail, which you passed on the Coxey Pond Trail. Turn left.

The trail goes through a wet area with inset logs, then up and over several rocky knobs. At a T-intersection, turn right onto the North Star Run. The trail descends and ascends along a rocky ravine and you pass between two large boulders. Next comes a high wall of rock on your right. You pass through tall pines. The trail makes a short, steep descent and is very rocky in spots.

Turn left at the next intersection to head back to the Sentinels, then retrace your steps to the parking area.

24

Temperance River State Park

Total distance: 2.5 miles

Approximate hiking time: 1.5 hours

Difficulty: Easy

Vertical rise: 250 feet

Maps: USGS 7½' Schroeder quad, Minnesota Department of Natural Resources state park map

The Ojibwe called this river *kawimbash* or "deep hollow" river. Over thousands of years, the water cut through basalt lava flows left during Minnesota's volcanic period 1.2 billion years ago. The rapidly moving water caught stones, pebbles, and sand in endless whirlpools that carved larger and larger potholes into the rock. Eventually, the potholes got so big that they joined together to form this narrow gorge. Other potholes were exposed when the river changed course. As the river squeezes through the high walls of the scenic gorge, it shoots out in many waterfalls and rapids.

An 1874 geological report records the name Temperance River. Thomas Clark, assistant state geologist, explained that most streams entering Lake Superior were "nearly closed at their mouth by gravel, called the bar, thrown up by the lake's waves. This stream, never having a 'bar' at its entrance, to incommode and baffle the weary voyageur in securing a safe landing, is called no *bar* or Temperance river."

The Temperance River is a designated trout stream. Over the years, brook, brown, and rainbow trout, as well as chinook salmon and steelhead have been stocked in the river and its vicinity.

The trees in this small park are similar to those that grew before white settlers arrived. White and yellow birch, white pine, spruce, fir, and cedar are prevalent.

Only 200 acres, the area became a state park in 1957. Facilities include a campsite with 55 semimodern spaces, 18 with elec-

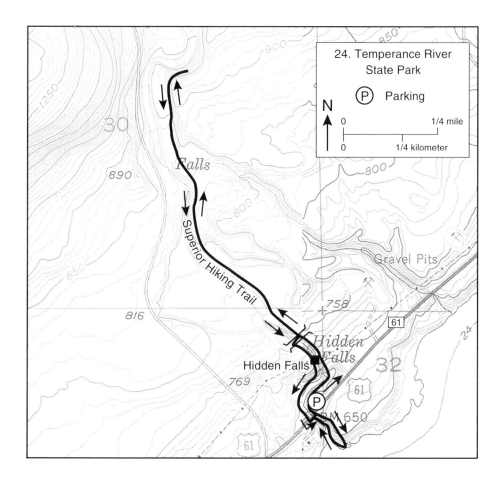

24. Temperance River
State Park

Ⓟ Parking

N

0   1/4 mile

0   1/4 kilometer

tricity. Restrooms and showers are located in the upper campground, on the north side of the river. Three cart-in campsites also are available. The lower campground has a picnic area. Contact the state park at 218-663-7476.

Carlton Peak, to the northeast, also is part of the state park. This large block of erosion-resistant anorthosite was carried up on the magma that forms the North Shore. Glaciers later scraped away the surrounding volcanic rock, leaving the distinctive knob that stands alone from a distance. Commercial fisherman used the point for navigation at the turn of the 20th century. The 924-foot-high peak can be reached by continuing the hike described here.

How to Get There

From Duluth, drive 81 miles northeast on MN 61. There are two parking areas right on the roadway. Use the larger one, just north of the Temperance River.

The Trail

The trail starts on the west side of the highway, at the north end of the highway bridge over the river. Look for the Cauldron Trail sign.

The Temperance River flows through a rocky gorge

The trail follows the river where it flows through a relatively flat, open area. The packed dirt trail curves right, along with the river as it flows over football-size rocks. Up ahead you can see the rocky cliffs where the river constricts and flows through the canyon.

The river turns left as the trail joins the Superior Hiking Trail, where you also turn left. Pass a trail on your right that heads back to MN 61. Head up the cliffs. Low stone walls line the clifftops, and signs explain the geology of the river gorge. There are no guardrails, so be careful.

Continue up the rock ledge, using rock steps and small boulders. As the large rock outcrop flattens, stay to the left. The narrow canyon squeezes the river into a fast-running chute that cascades down several outcrops forming small waterfalls, including one called Hidden Falls. Pass another trail to the right that goes to the highway by the park's information office.

Come to a heavy metal bridge high over the river. Continue upriver, following the Temperance River and Hiking Club signs. Descend some rock steps to another overlook with a low stone wall. At the overlook marked with the number 7, you are 240 feet above the level of Lake Superior.

Descend steps down from the high ledges. Here, just above the narrow canyon, the river still flows over rocky outcrops, but the area is wider. To the north, the river valley starts to open even wider, and the woods start coming in to meet the rocky banks.

Pass a trail that comes in from the right. Here the level trail widens and continues through the mixed, open birch forest with shrubby underbrush and the occasional pine. The river is lined on either side with large rocks and boulders, which allow hikers to walk out into the stream.

About 1.2 miles from the start of this hike, the trail ascends and you come to the Hiking Club password sign and a bench. From here, the Superior Hiking Trail continues to Carlton Peak, 2 miles to the northeast.

We turned around and headed back to the bridge and crossed to the west side of the river. Here you can see potholes carved over thousands of years by swirling sand and pebbles. One is large enough to hold a dozen hikers. The dry potholes were exposed after the river moved to a different course.

Continue downriver toward MN 61 and Lake Superior. Cross the highway, which can be very busy during the summer. Just across the road is a bridge on the east side pedestrian path. At the end of the bridge, turn right at a sign that reads "trail." Descend about 20 wooden steps. A left leads to the park's information office and an intersection with a trail to the upper campground. Continue straight ahead then head to your right, down to the lake on a trail that includes many steps and broad landings. The north side ends at a rocky outcrop covered with orange lichen.

A bridge crosses the narrow gorge, and you can explore both sides. There might not have been a sandbar hundreds of years ago, but today's Temperance River flows through the rocky cliffs and meets a narrow strip of sand at Lake Superior.

25

Tettegouche State Park

Total distance: 11.6 miles

Approximate hiking time: 6 hours, 15 minutes

Difficulty: Moderate; steep in many places

Vertical rise: 1,000 feet

Maps: USGS 7½' Illgen City quad, Minnesota Department of Natural Resources state park map

This park has two of the most spectacularly rugged points on the 1.2-billion-year-old lava flows that make up the North Shore. Shovel Point is a thick, red rhyolite point that sits above Lake Superior. High cliffs edge this intrusion into the basalt of a previous lava flow, and arches and caves gouge the rock where it meets the lake. About 2 miles southwest of the park is 200-foot-high Palisade Head, which can be seen from Shovel Point.

West of Lake Superior, the Baptism River flows through a rocky gorge in a series of waterfalls and cascades. The highest waterfall entirely within Minnesota is located here. More than 20 ancient gray basalt and red rhyolite lava flows have been identified within 2 miles upstream from the highway.

The park's interior contains rugged ridges surrounding six small inland lakes. Scenic overlooks abound along the park's 23 miles of hiking trails. Mount Trudee is a large, erosion-resistant dome.

Scenic beauty wasn't the area's first attraction. It was trees. Loggers set up camp on the shores of what they called Mic Mac Lake, after Native Americans in their native New Brunswick, about 1898. When the giant red and white pine had been logged off in 1910, the logging company sold the camp to a group of Duluth business owners known as the Tettegouche Club. Two private owners continued a tradition of land stewardship until a state park was established in 1979. The four log cabins have been restored. Park visitors can rent the cabins, which can be reached only on foot.

Coniferous Forests

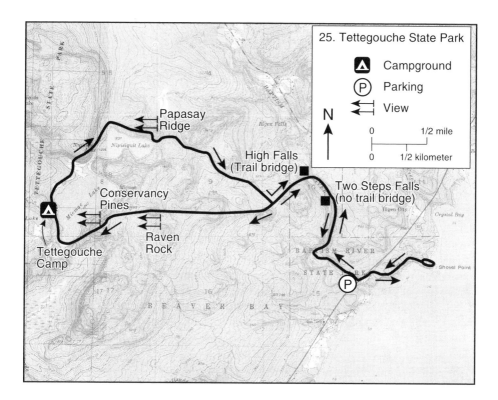

The park also offers diverse vegetation. Cedar and black ash wetlands—along with stands of aspen and birch—lie along the Baptism River, west of Lake Superior, in an area that previously was completely logged and burned. At the higher elevation of the inland lakes, mature sugar maple, yellow birch, basswood, and white spruce abruptly replace the aspen and birch. Still higher, on the dry ridgetops, scattered red and white pine and red oak can be found.

In addition to the restored Tettegouche Camp cabins, the park has a campground with 34 semimodern sites, flush toilets, and showers. A campground where visitors use lightweight carts to haul in equipment and supplies has 13 sites. Two group campsites also are available. Four backpack campsites are located along the Superior Hiking Trail as it runs through the park, and one kayak camp-site is on the lakeshore. The park also has four picnic areas and a visitor center with exhibits on history, geology, and vegetation. The park's phone number is 218-226-6365.

The main hike described here goes to High Falls and into the park's interior, but it's worth heading out to Shovel Point first. This is a 1-mile hike with interpretive signs, and several sets of stairs. We won't describe it in detail; it's easy to follow the trail. Rock climbers were heading over the cliff, and kayakers were paddling far below the day we visited. The view at the end of the point is magnificent.

How to Get There

From Duluth, drive 58 miles northeast on US 61, past Silver Bay. The state park and highway rest area entrance on the east side of the road is well marked.

The Trail

This park has well-marked trails that use a letter system at intersections. Lots of ascents and descents—many with steps—over rugged terrain and six overlooks make this a full day of hiking. Of course, you don't have to check out all the scenic spots and can keep plugging away at the trail. However, we recommend packing plenty of food and water, and taking your time.

Park in the visitor center lot. After checking out Shovel Point, head to the visitor center and turn left, walking on the park road for little more than 0.1 mile. At another parking area, look for the High Falls Trail sign on the west side. Ascend some steps and head under MN 61 with the river to your left. Climb about 29 more steps to another trail sign. Continue on the High Falls Trail, which is packed dirt.

For the next 1 mile the trail goes over rocks and roots, crosses wet areas via boardwalks, and ascends and descends many, many steps. We tried to keep count and came up with more than 250 steps in varying combinations on the hike upriver to High Falls. The forest is mostly birch of varying ages and density. Some small areas of pine are enclosed to keep deer from eating the young seedlings.

At Two Step Falls, a trail that will connect to the Superior Hiking Trail northeast of the river heads off to the right. Continue toward High Falls, the highest in Minnesota at 70 feet. Pigeon Falls in Grand Portage State Park is higher, but shared with Canada.

A spur trail leads down to the base of the falls. Cross a suspension bridge built by the Minnesota Department of Natural Resources and the Superior Hiking Trail Asso-

Rugged Lake Superior shoreline at Tettegouche State Park

Coniferous Forests

ciation. Ascend steps to an overlook of the falls and continue onto the Superior Hiking Trail. At intersection B continue straight ahead. In about 0.1 mile is the first overlook. Pass through an intersection with the Tettegouche Trail, a snowmobile trail, and up through the Drainpipe, a 150-foot gash with rock steps.

In about 0.8 mile is intersection C, where you continue straight ahead on the Superior Hiking Trail and on to the Raven Rock overlook spur. Continue through a low area and over a bridge to intersection L, where the Superior Hiking Trail heads south toward Mount Trudee and Lake Superior. Shortly, a spur trail to your right leads to the Conservancy Pines overlook, a small ledge with towering red pines.

The trail continues toward Mic Mac Lake and curves around its southern tip. A trail at intersection I leads left to Palisade Valley and Floating Bog Bay overlooks, then continues to the park's boundary. Head that way if you're not overlooked-out.

Back at intersection I, head toward Tettegouche Camp. Pass another trail to Floating Bog Bay to your left, then the park road that leads to a parking area along Lake County 4. This is where visitors can park when they walk in to stay at the Tettegouche cabins. Another trail leads to Nicado Lake. Pass them all, walking through the cabins and staying to the left, at Cabin C, along Mic Mac Lake.

Cross a bridge over Mosquito Creek and continue toward Nipisiquit Lake. At intersection E, continue straight ahead. Stay to your right at the next intersection with a narrow trail up to Papasay Ridge. A spur trail gives a view of the Sawtooth Mountains to the west. Continue past the other end of the Papasay Ridge bypass, a picnic table, and a snowmobile trail to your left to intersection D. The Tettegouche Trail intersects the trail. Stay to your left.

In about 0.3 mile is the intersection with the Lake Superior overlook spur trail. From here the main trail, marked "more difficult," descends back to intersection B and the Superior Hiking Trail.

Here you can return to the High Falls, cross the bridge, and continue downriver the way you came. Or if you've had enough step-climbing for the day, pass over the Superior Hiking Trail to the trailhead parking area. It's about 1.1 miles down the winding road to MN 61, and another 0.1 mile back to the main parking areas.

26

Vermilion Gorge Trail

Total distance: 3 miles

Approximate hiking time: 1.5 hours

Difficulty: Moderate

Vertical rise: 60 feet

Maps: USGS 7½' Johnson Lake quad, USDA Forest Service map

The Vermilion River flows from the lake of the same name over a waterfall and through a narrow gorge before it enters Crane Lake 38 miles north. The river and lake name comes from a translation of the Ojibwe *on-amuni*, which referred to the red reflections of the setting sun. This apparently is the same name origin of the much larger Red Lake, more than 100 miles to the west.

Minnesota's lakes and rivers were the pathways of Native Americans as they moved throughout the region to hunt, fish, and gather other food. As French explorers and fur traders moved into northern Minnesota, they either adopted or were guided along these routes. Frenchman René Bourassa operated a trading post at the mouth of the river on Crane Lake in 1736. From there, voyageurs could travel on the 3,000-mile waterway connecting the commercial hub of Montreal with the fur-rich area of Lake Athabasca in northwestern Canada.

Vermilion Lake also was the site of an iron ore discovery in 1865. That same year, the Vermilion Lake Gold Rush was touched off by reports of the valuable mineral in quartz samples taken near the northeastern shore. A year later, 300 people were living at the lake and mining for gold. It never was found, but the rich veins of iron ore were confirmed and the "entombed iron giant" was released. In the ancient rocks of the Vermilion Range, the ores were the hard type, found in complex, deep-pitched troughs.

Loggers also came to the area in the early 1900s.

Coniferous Forests

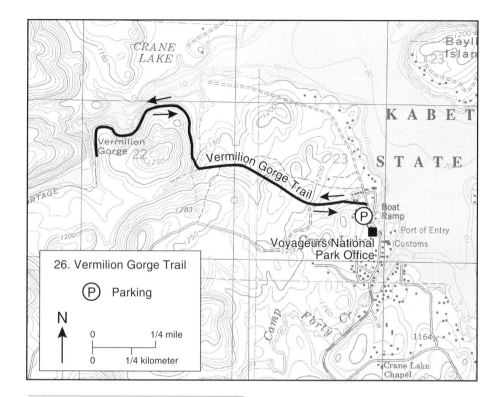

How to Get There

Crane Lake is about 4 miles from the Canadian border. From Virginia, head north on US 53 about 42 miles to Orr. Head northeast on St. Louis County 23 about 15 miles to Buyck. Head north on St. Louis County 24 for about 10 miles, literally to the end of the road, in Crane Lake.

The Trail

Drive to the north end of Crane Lake. A small Voyageurs National Park station is located on the west side of the road, just before a bar, restaurant, and lodge. The station's telephone number is 218-993-2481. The trailhead is located in an odd spot—the parking lot across from this business. Walk along the north edge of the parking lot, which was jam-packed with vehicles

pulling boat trailers. Look for the brown and white National Forest Hiking Trail sign.

Once you're past the hubbub of the lodge, the gravel trail ascends and passes through wooden pillars set into the ground. The first section has interpretive signs about the fur trade and logging.

The trail makes a long descent with about 20 widely spaced timbers set in as steps. Boardwalks cross wet areas, and the dense understory of the birch and aspen forest overgrows the trail in one area.

This is where a small, round black shape ran parallel to the trail just within the trees. As Baby Bear bounded further into the woods, we hoped Mama Bear wasn't close by. Following the advice posted at the ranger station, we made more noise to announce our presence to any other bears.

The gorge on the Vermilion River

About 0.75 mile from the start, the trail meets the Vermilion River, which is down a steep bank to your right. The trail makes several steep descents and ascents with steps, then you come to a wide floating dock. Standing on the bobbing surface gives you a good view of this wide section of river. Head up some large rocks to your right to pick up the trail. Here the forest changes to open stands of red pine with moss-covered boulders and forest-floor plants like bunchberry. The settings are picture-perfect scenes of the North Woods.

Continue up the steep footpath, which is covered with rocks and roots. As you ascend above the river, look down on its banks, which are starting to narrow into flat, rocky ledges. You reach the top of a rocky knob with the cliffs of the gorge falling straight down. The view is great, but there are no railings, and it's a long way down. The trail ends at a large rock wall to your left. The scene westward from the edge of the gorge is the river spread out in a marshy plain. A few miles upstream the river shoots through a narrow gap named Vermilion Falls.

Coniferous Forests

27

Voyageurs National Park

Total distance: 3.6 miles

Approximate hiking time: 1 hour, 45 minutes

Difficulty: Easy to moderate

Vertical rise: Minimal

Maps: USGS 7½' Ash River NE quad, National Park Service map

The first inhabitants of what is now Voyageurs National Park gave the landscape many of the names still used today. Namakan, Kabetogama, and Nashata Lakes come from the Ojibwe language. These people lived on the lakes' shores, spearing fish and harvesting wild rice.

French explorers may have reached the hinterlands beyond Lake Superior as early as 1688, when a voyageur named Jacques de Noyon seems to have spent a winter at Rainy Lake. Cryptic notations on early maps and other records indicate the French were in the area at this time.

The Canadian-born Pierre Gaultier de Varennes, Sieur de la Vérendrye, came looking for a route to the "Sea of the West" after hearing Native Americans tell of a river that flowed into a salt sea. In 1731, la Vérendrye set out with three sons and a small expedition. It took two months to reach what would become the famed fur trade post of Grand Portage. From there, several members of the party continued on to Rainy Lake and built a post called Fort St. Pierre. By 1733, the French had pushed farther west, and canoes began traveling the open water highway of lakes and rivers along the future international border.

French-Canadian canoe paddlers became the human conveyor belt, moving goods and pelts. Using Native Americans as guides and suppliers, voyageurs paddled up to 16 hours a day, transporting trade goods and supplies into the subarctic interior of northwest Canada and bringing furs out to Lake Superior posts. The round trip between

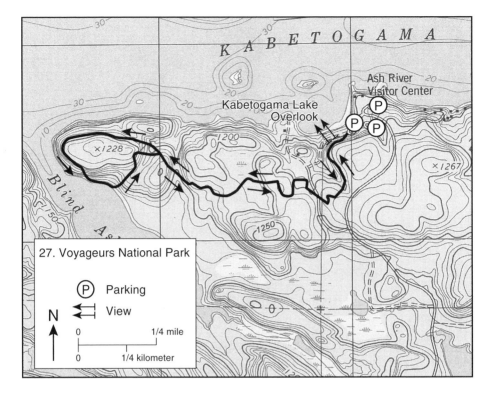

K A B E T O G A M A

Ash River
Visitor Center

Kabetogama Lake
Overlook

×1228

×1267

Blind As

1200

1250

27. Voyageurs National Park

P Parking

N View

0   1/4 mile

0   1/4 kilometer

Grand Portage and the fur-gathering interior took four or five months.

These were the winterers, or Nor'westers, according to Theodore Blegen's history of Minnesota. They traveled in canoes that could hold up to 3,000 pounds of goods and an eight-man crew, smaller than those used on the Great Lakes.

The colorful history of the voyageurs usually notes their strength, endurance, and dress, which was somewhat flamboyant for guys who sat in canoes or trotted through forests all day. A typical outfit consisted of a bright blue capote, red cap, braided sash, leggings, and deerskin moccasins. "And, if he had achieved the proud status of a Nor'wester, a plume," Blegen wrote.

Singing also was a big part of a voyageur's life, and songs were adapted to provide a rhythm for paddling. The voyageurs apparently didn't sing about the wilderness, preferring "songs about nightingales, cavaliers, springtime, rosebuds, fair ladies, and gallant captains."

Glacial movement caused the depressions and beds that became the lakes and rivers the voyageurs traveled. Granite, biotite, schist, migmatite, and a small area of greenstone about 2.7 billion years old underlie the park. The rocky knobs and ridges providing the stark backdrop to the park's wilderness vistas are some of the world's oldest exposed rock formations.

A National Park first was suggested in 1891, but decades of wrangling about boundaries and land use put the proposal on a shelf. When US 53 was completed in 1922, tourists began coming to the area in greater numbers. The US government authorized establishment of the park in 1971,

Coniferous Forests

Kabetogama Lake

and Voyageurs National Park became a reality in 1975. More than 40 logging camps operated in the park area during the industry's peak from 1907 to 1929, so most of the big trees are gone.

You would expect a park named to commemorate the voyageurs to have lots of water, and it does. Of the park's 218,055 acres, almost 84,000 are water. More than 30 large and small lakes—along with bogs, marshes, and beaver ponds—are located within its boundaries.

That doesn't mean hikers are lacking for opportunities. Thirteen hiking trails range from 0.25 mile to 24 miles long. Six of the trails can be reached only by water, but access to the remaining seven is on land. The park has four entry points, but this hike starts from the Ash River Visitor Center, which is open seasonally. The historic log lodge contains exhibits and other information. The telephone number is 218-374-3221.

How to Get There

Voyageurs National Park is a six-hour drive from Minneapolis–St. Paul or three hours from Duluth. From Virginia, head north about 65 miles through the villages of Orr and Cusson. Head east on St. Louis County 129, which ends at the Ash River Visitor Center 8 miles down the road.

The Trail

Park in the lower lot. That way you can check out the historic log lodge that houses the visitor center, where toilets and water are located. This spot, with its incredible view of Kabetogama Lake and its small islands, must have seemed like a slice of heaven to the private owners who lived at this isolated cabin before the park was established.

The park literature says that this hike is 2.5 miles long, but we measured it at about 3.6 miles. The park worker we asked agreed it's longer than printed material indicates.

Head to the upper parking area to the Blind Ash Bay Hiking Trail sign, on the western edge. Walk up 11 wooden steps, then up a moderately steep, rocky footpath. At the Kabetogama Lake overlook is one of those lush North Woods areas of moss, lichen, forest floor plants, and pine that you swear has been arranged by a photo stylist.

Past this mossy spot, the narrow, rocky, and root-covered trail ascends slightly. An area of exposed rock interrupts the footpath, so look to your left to pick up the trail. Cross a Park Service road. There are no signs on this trail section. The forest here is widely spaced birch and some pine, with an understory of ferns.

A boardwalk crosses a boggy area. Pass a bench. The trail descends, then goes up some rocks that were slippery from a light rain. The trail ascends with a switchback curve.

Come to a sign marking the start of the Blind Ash Bay loop. Head to your right and begin climbing up rocks and boulders. A bench overlooks the lake and several small islands. The trail then turns left to follow the bay and descends through an area of mossy boulders. Keep descending until you're within 20 feet of the shoreline. The trail is very rocky in spots. Soon the trail curves left again and ascends through an area of old pine. Next is a section of fallen trees, to your left.

Ascending to the top of the rise brings you back to the start of the loop. A tall pine provided shelter from a heavy downpour, and the wet trail slowed the pace as we retraced our steps back to the parking area.

Deciduous Forests

Sand Creek in Louisville Swamp

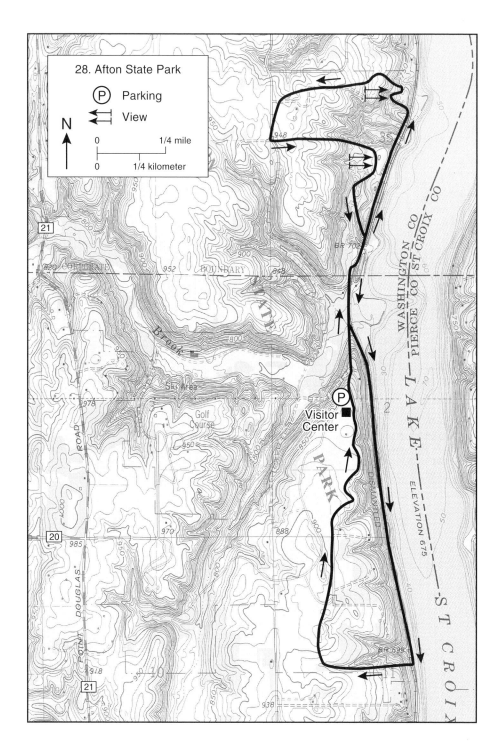

28. Afton State Park

P Parking

View

N

0 .... 1/4 mile

0 .... 1/4 kilometer

28

Afton State Park

Total distance: 6.5 miles

Approximate hiking time: 4 hours

Difficulty: Moderate

Vertical rise: 300 feet

Maps: USGS 7½' Prescott quad, Minnesota Department of Natural Resources state park map

Afton State Park lies along the bluffs of the St. Croix River. Forested ravines, with jutting outcrops of sandstone, descend 300 feet to the river in places. On the park's western border, Afton Alps Ski Area takes advantage of the terrain.

The Aftons in this area—state park, township, town, and ski area—take their names from a poem, "Afton Water," by Scottish poet Robert Burns. Apparently, the area brought the poem to mind for a local founder.

> How lofty, sweet Afton, thy neighboring hills
> Far marked with the courses of clear winding rills
> There daily I wander as noon rises high
> My flocks and my Mary's sweet cot in my eye.

The Afton Water of Burns's poem is a stream in Scotland. The water of Afton State Park is the St. Croix River, a designated Wild and Scenic River.

The prairies on the blufftops used to be farm fields but are being restored. This state park is built around nature-oriented recreation. Development has been minimized, and most facilities can be reached only by trails. It's an uphill hike of 0.75 mile to the 24-site main campground, although roads lead to two rustic group camps. One canoe campsite also is located at the swimming area. The park's phone number is 651-436-5391.

How to Get There

From St. Paul, head 9 miles east on I-94. Turn south on MN 95 for 7 miles, then east 3 miles on Washington County Road 20. The park entrance is at the intersection with Washington County Road 21. The park office is located on prairie that had beautiful, 4-foot-tall big bluestem grass waving orange when we visited in late August. The road winds about 1.5 miles past the office to parking for all facilities except the group camps.

The Trail

This park has 20 miles of hiking trails with several multiple-trail intersections that can be confusing. The St. Croix makes a good reference point, so if think you're off the route described here and can get a peek of water, head toward it. You should end up on the main north-south artery.

Start this hike at the northernmost parking loop near the visitor center. Look for the Hiking Club sign and follow the paved trail through the picnic area for about 0.2 mile to an overlook on your right. Here you get a broad view of the river. Migrating hawks and eagles use the St. Croix and Mississippi riverways.

After leaving the overlook, descend a number of stairs, about 85 interspersed between broad landings. Stay on the Hiking Club Trail at the next intersection. You'll cross a bridge over Trout Creek, then at about 0.5 mile into this hike come to the swimming beach along the river. Turn right to check out the river. You can walk along its banks, then find a path that leads back up to the main trail. This is an old railroad bed that parallels the river in a straight line, with cottonwood and silver maple alongside, to the northern park boundary.

About 1.2 miles into this hike, a bench sits at a trail intersection. Continue straight ahead to where the trail turns to your left. Here you begin ascending the bluff, among the ravines covered with oak, aspen, and birch. A short level area breaks up two steep climbs.

Open prairie sits at the top of the bluff. Next comes a potentially confusing five-way trail intersection. A trail that angles sharply left takes you to an overlook of the river. Check it out, then head back to the intersection and take the trail that goes mostly straight ahead, but slightly to the left. Shortly you pass a trail to the right, which is a loop that goes back to the five-way intersection.

Continue on the wide mowed path as it curves south, to your left, and comes to a trail intersection with a park shelter. Continue straight ahead. At the next four-way intersection, turn left toward the river. Going straight ahead takes you to the hike-in campground.

The trail descends gently, then steeply, through a small section of pine. Next is an area of mixed prairie and woods along the bluff, with another scenic overlook before a final steep descent to the river.

At the river, the trail goes under a footbridge before joining the old railroad bed trail at the swimming area. Turn right and continue until you come to another multitrail intersection. Stay to the left, back on the Hiking Club Trail, which heads up the stairs to the lookout and parking area shortly.

Continue hiking along the river, passing through another picnic area with sidewalks before joining up with the packed-dirt trail. For the next 1.3 miles the trail hugs the river with a maple forest sloping up to a steep sandstone cliff on your right. Small ravines that carry runoff water cut through the slope.

The trail turns right and ascends the bluff, where a bench sits at the top of another open prairie. Turn right on the grass path at the next intersection, continue past a park shelter, and cross a gravel road that leads to the group camp. Here you enter an area of jack and red pine before crossing a gravel road to a second group campsite.

The trail winds left and right and up and down several gentle hills, then comes to another river overlook. The trail curves left and meets the paved biking trail in a little over 0.1 mile.

Turn right and continue past an area of prairie restoration to your left. The next intersection is an 0.8-mile loop, marked with a Hiking Club sign, through this area of prairie.

After completing the loop, turn left onto the biking trail again. The park's visitor center, with interpretive displays on habitat and wildlife, is to your right. Past the center, the paved trail continues to the parking area.

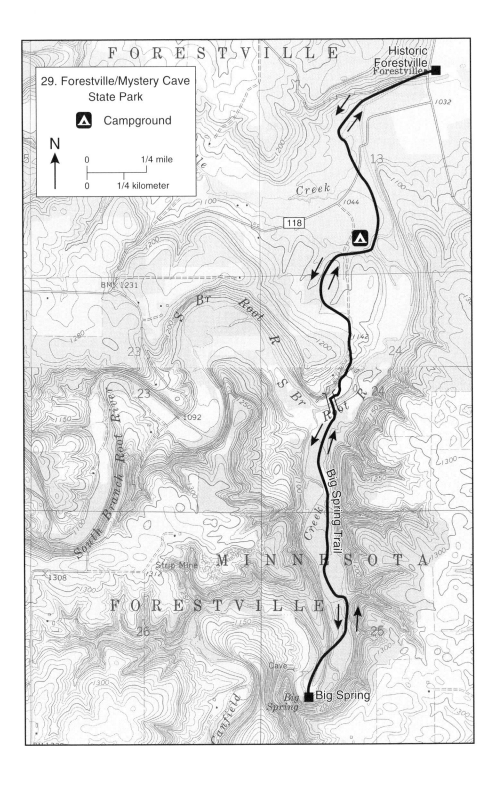

Historic
Forestville

29. Forestville/Mystery Cave
State Park

▲ Campground

N

0   1/4 mile

0   1/4 kilometer

Creek

118

13

1032

1100

1044

1100

1200

Br

Root

R

S

Br

BM 1231

1280

1200

23

23

1092

1200

1142

1200

24

Root R. 24

1300

1250

1300

South Branch Root River

250

1100

100

Big Spring Trail

Creek

1150

1308

1312

Strip Mine

M I N N E S O T A

1300

1300

F O R E S T V I L L E

26

1150

25

1300

1200

1300

1300

Cave

1300

Big
Spring

■ Big Spring

Cranfield

29

Forestville/Mystery Cave State Park

Total distance: 7.6 miles

Approximate hiking time: 3.5 hours

Difficulty: Easy

Vertical rise: Minimal

Maps: USGS 7½' Forestville and Greenleafton quads, Minnesota Department of Natural Resources state park map

This state park encompasses a recreated 1890s village and Minnesota's longest cave. The cave is part of Minnesota's karst geology. Such an area occurs in soluble rock like limestone when water moves down through the water table, picking up carbon dioxide from decaying organic material. The mild carbonic acid that results can dissolve minerals in the stone. Over many thousands of years, caves and sinkholes, the typical karst features, develop. Fillmore County, where this state park is located, is dotted with sinkholes.

Forestville/Mystery Cave State Park also is on the edge of Minnesota's "driftless" region. The last glaciers that covered other parts of the state didn't make it to the southeastern corner. Little debris, or drift, is left from the older glaciers, and the region lacks the rolling hills that mark more glaciated areas of the state. However, powerful glacial meltwater created the steep hills and bluffs of the Mississippi River valley. You can see these formations along the park's eastern and northern borders.

The sides of these bluffs have differing microclimates. Slopes facing north are cooler and wetter, south-facing slopes warmer and drier. The state's prairie also meets the eastern deciduous forest in the park, creating great diversity in plants that in turn support a large variety of bird species. Scarlet tanagers, ovenbirds, redstarts, wild turkeys, barred owls, and turkey vultures have been seen.

With three spring-fed streams, the park also is noted for trout fishing. Other park

Source of the Big Spring

facilities include a campsite with 73 semi-modern sites—23 with electricity, a trailer dumping station with showers and flush toilets, a large picnic area with an enclosed shelter, a summer interpretive amphitheater, a horseback rider camp, and, of course, Mystery Cave. Contact the park by calling 507-352-5111.

How to Get There

Forestville/Mystery Cave State Park is about 30 miles south of Rochester. From just north of the Preston city limit, head west on MN 16 for about 9 miles. Turn south on Fillmore County 5 for about 3 miles to Fillmore County 118. Turn east, and drive 2 miles to the park entrance.

The Trail

Continue on the main park road to the parking area for historic Forestville. Walk toward the old village from the northeast corner of the lot. At the white picket fence at the edge of the house's yard, turn left. Because no other people were in sight when we arrived, watching the costumed interpreter come out of the house to dump a pail of water really was like stepping back in time.

The trail enters the wooded area. This section also is used by horseback riders and is a wide, packed-dirt path. A creek is to your left, and several very large cottonwoods grow along its banks. You walk along the base of a steep bluff. At a Y-intersection marked with a map, turn left. Keep the creek to your left, as you will also turn that direction at the next intersection. Soon you cross Forestville Creek over large, rectangular stepping-stones. Cross the park road and continue straight ahead on a hiking-only trail. The trail has remnants of wood chips and passes through an area with lots of white snakeroot.

The trail now follows the South Branch of the Root River to the campground. Turn left

on the road and walk about 0.1 mile to a trail sign kiosk with a water fountain. A bridge to your left goes over a ravine that connects to another trail.

Cross the intersection of park roads, heading toward the trailer station, and look for the hiking-only trail to your left. The forest here is very tall maple and multistemmed cottonwood. The trail continues through the woods over a curved boardwalk for about 0.5 mile. You come to a mowed, open area of sumac and some pine with hills rising to your right. Continue straight ahead to an intersection with the Maple Ridge Trail. Turn left and cross the park road.

The gravel trail descends and ascends moderately through an area of pine. Soon you see the Root River to your left. At a sign that reads NO HORSES, turn left and walk down about 40 log steps to a boardwalk. A level mowed grass path leads to the river through 8-foot-tall Jerusalem artichokes and joe-pye weed. The hiking and horse trails reconnect, and an opening in the riverside vegetation allows horses to cross. Climb the steps to cross the pedestrian bridge, then turn right. The trail hugs the river, which curves to the right where it is joined by Canfield Creek.

The destination of this trail section is the Big Spring. For the next 1.4 miles the trail is level through a mixed maple and basswood forest, dotted with some pine. Spotted jewelweed, star chickweed, asters, goldenrod, and sunflowers were blooming during our August hike.

This section of trail requires two creek crossings. You can step on rocks in the first small stream without getting your feet wet, but the second crossing was through water 1.5 feet deep. On the way to Big Spring, we crossed barefoot over very sharp rocks through icy cold water. On the way back, we crossed in our hiking shoes. Wet feet were preferable to injured feet. You also could carry a pair of light sandals for the creek crossing.

The trail ends at a spectacular limestone cliff with a small opening at its base. After percolating down through the cliff, water flows out of the hole as Canfield Creek. The water flows out slowly, but a horseback rider told us it gushed out years ago. She wondered if the decrease in water is due to dry weather or loss of wetlands due to land development.

After taking in the cool air in the shadow of the bluff and the view of steep wooded hills farther east, retrace your steps back to historic Forestville. There are several places where you meet and can walk back along the park roads if you prefer.

Bonus Destinations

Forestville was a typical Minnesota village in the late 1850s. It was named in honor of Henry Forest, Fillmore County's first probate judge and one of the village's founders. Farmers brought crops to the gristmill and traded produce for goods and services at the two general stores. A brickyard, two hotels, and a school operated in the small town. Twenty buildings with 100 people made up the town in 1858. When the first area railroad bypassed Forestville ten years later, the struggle for survival began. By 1890, Thomas Meighen owned the entire village. Most of the remaining 50 residents worked on his farm, in his store, or in his house in exchange for housing and store credit. The last residents of Forestville left in 1910, leaving the buildings and the Meighen family store stocked with merchandise. The Minnesota Historical Society operates a restored section of the village, including Meighen's house and general store. Costumed interpreters work as store clerks, housemaids, gardeners, and farmhands. Cooks prepare meals in the working 19th-century kitchen. The site is open Memorial Day through Labor Day, and an admission fee is charged.

Mystery Cave has 12 miles of passages in two rock layers. Typical speleothems like bacon strips, flowstone, stalactites and stalagmites, as well as blue pools of water and fossils can be seen. The cave entrance is on the west side of Fillmore County 5, about 5.5 miles south of the main park. Guided tours are given every day during summer and on weekends in spring and fall. A state park vehicle permit is required, and admission also is charged.

30

Interstate State Park

Total distance: 3.5 miles

Approximate hiking time: 2 hours, 15 minutes

Difficulty: Moderate

Vertical rise: 250 feet

Maps: USGS 7½' St. Croix Dalles quad, Minnesota Department of Natural Resources state park map

No, this park isn't located along a freeway. The name refers to the joint venture with Wisconsin that created parks on either side of the St. Croix River. Interstate preserves some of Minnesota's most interesting and beautiful geologic features. The dark gray basalt cliffs probably were formed by the same ancient volcanic eruptions responsible for the North Shore of Lake Superior. Later, the lava flows were covered by sedimentary rocks about 575 millions years later. Next came the glaciers. As they thawed, meltwater rushed south in a large stream, carving the ancestral St. Croix valley. The erosion-resistant basalts withstood the watery assault, forming the scenic Dalles of the St. Croix River we see today.

Another geologic feature found in the park is large glacial potholes that formed when whirlpools swirled sand round and round carving into the bedrock. Some of the potholes are large enough to stand in. The largest is over 60 feet deep.

A third area of interest is Curtain Falls, where thousands of years of erosion has cut an amphitheater-like bowl in the sandstone. Unfortunately, a torrential rainstorm collapsed part of the trail at the falls in 2003.

The Dalles of the St. Croix have been a tourist attraction for many years. Steamboat service to the city of Taylors Falls, which meets the park's northern border, began in 1838. Iron mooring rings can be seen in the rock along the river.

Before modern times, the St. Croix River was a major waterway used by Native Americans, French, British, and American

The St. Croix River

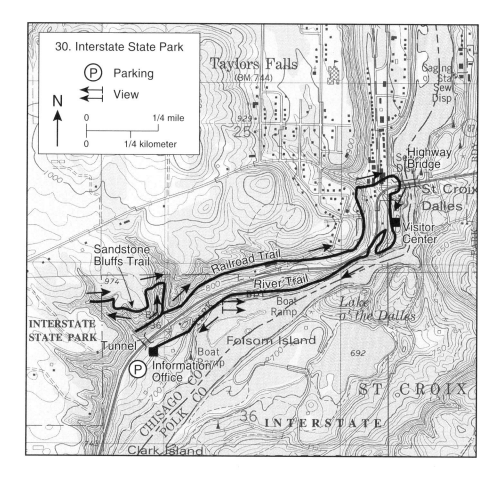

30. Interstate State Park

- (P) Parking
- View

N

0 — 1/4 mile
0 — 1/4 kilometer

explorers and traders, and loggers. Logs were transported downriver to sawmills, but often caught in massive jams at the rocky Dalles. Once in 1886, logs were jammed 7 miles up the river.

The St. Croix was designed a Wild and Scenic River in 1968. This means the river must be "preserved in free-flowing condition" with its immediate environment also protected.

This is a small park, only 293 acres. Its deep ravines and valleys are forested with maple, basswood, and some pine. Oak savanna also occurs in the park.

Facilities include a campground with 37 semimodern sites, 22 of which have electricity, a primitive group camp, picnic area with two shelters, a visitor center and nature store, and a trailer sanitation station with flush toilets and showers. Canoes can be rented. The park's telephone number is 651-465-5711.

How to Get There

From Minneapolis–St. Paul head north on I-35 about 19 miles to Forest Lake. Head northeast on MN 8 for another 19 miles. The park is located just south of Taylors Falls, with its entrance on the east side of the road.

The Trail

Park at the information office/park head-quarters. Just south of the building a trail heads west. Descend several steps and cross through a tunnel under the highway. It's low, so watch your head.

Come to an intersection with the Sand-stone Bluffs Trail, which was closed in this area when we hiked. Fourteen inches of rain rushed through the gully below Curtain Falls in the spring of 2003, collapsing the trail and toppling trees. Ask at the park office if this section of trail has been reopened.

Instead, turn right toward the Railroad Trail. There are numerous steps to climb and descend. At the bottom of a long stairway to the top of the Railroad Trail, turn left and head into the ravine above a small creek. Cross a bridge over the creek. For the next 0.3 mile, the trail goes up several steep inclines with wooden timbers set in as steps as you climb to the top of a bluff.

Steps and a wooden walkway lead to an overlook of bluffs and the river to the southeast. A sign provides information about the logging industry and its use of the St. Croix.

From the overlook, the narrow trail descends about 20 steps in hairpin turns, then continues down more steps. On your right is a moss-covered sandstone cliff. Descend stone steps and cross a bridge to Curtain Falls. The falls were dry when we last hiked here. This is the other end of the closed trail section. Just past the falls, you can see large trees over the trail. You have to retrace your steps back to the long flight of stairs on the railroad trail.

This time, turn left and climb the stairway. This trail follows the old railroad grade, partway along the base of a sandstone bluff, about 1.5 miles into Taylors Falls. You enter the town by the old railroad depot, an attractive building that has been renovated as a community center.

Follow the sidewalk past the depot and turn right on First Street. Follow the signs to the state park. It's a couple of city blocks to an overlook of the river on the north side of the street. Cross under a bridge past the scenic boat tours stand.

Trails to the potholes area lead from the south end of the visitor center parking lot. The view of the Dalles is spectacular along the river. After you've poked around the potholes for awhile, head back toward the parking lot and pick up the River Trail, which starts across from a drinking fountain.

Ascend some stone steps. A trail to the right leads to more potholes. Turn left and continue on the trail as steps ascend to MN 8. The trail parallels the highway for about 0.1 mile. The trail descends past a river overlook. The path is rocky and rooted here with several descents and ascents.

In about 0.4 mile another overlook gives a view of Folsom Island. You're walking closer to the river now, and a bridge crosses a wet area. At a Y-intersection marked with a sign, a trail to the campground leads to the left. Stay to the right. The trail passes through an area of young trees and past another path to your left. Take it and you cross a bridge as you curve back to the park office parking area.

31

Lake Maria State Park

Total distance: 4.5 miles

Approximate hiking time: 2 hours

Difficulty: Easy

Vertical rise: 80 feet

Maps: USGS 7½' Silver Creek quad, Minnesota Department of Natural Resources state park map

Lake Maria State Park contains remnants of the Big Woods that ran 100 miles long and 40 miles wide diagonally through Minnesota before settlers arrived. Some reports from the time say the sugar maple, basswood, elm, ash, and ironwood trees were so dense that sunlight didn't reach the forest floor. Today, only a small portion of the original 5,000 square miles of the Big Woods remains.

The park's topography is that of the St. Croix Moraine, a leftover of the 10,000-year-old Wisconsin Age glacier. A terminal moraine forms at the end of a glacial conveyor belt, where immense quantities of boulders, stones, gravel, and other sediment are dropped. In this park, glaciers dropped several feet of red, sandy till from around Lake Superior and clay and loam—sand, clay, silt, and organic matter—from the Red River valley. Underlying this soil is mostly granite bedrock.

The lake's name is pronounced ma·*rye*·uh. A park employee said the pronunciation is local, but he didn't know how it came about.

The woods interspersed with wetlands make this park good bird habitat. Vireos, flycatchers, ruffed grouse, red-shouldered hawks, and cerulean warblers live in the hardwoods. Ducks, loons, grebes, terns, and rails inhabit the lake and marsh areas.

The marshes also provide homes for the endangered Blanding's turtle, distinguished by its long, bright yellow neck and domed shell. Because this turtle closes up in a box shape, it's commonly called a box turtle, but

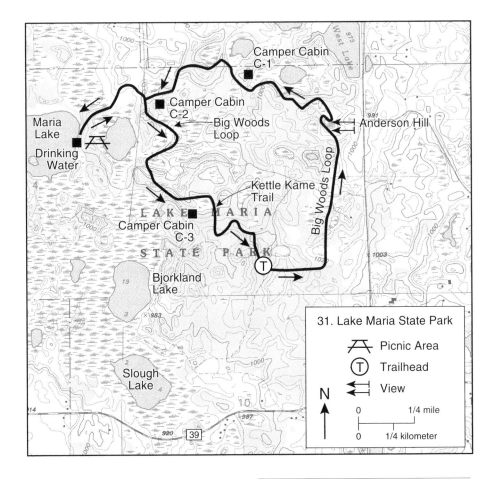

Maria Lake

Drinking Water

Camper Cabin C-1

Camper Cabin C-2

Big Woods Loop

Anderson Hill

Kettle Kame Trail

L A K E M A R I A

Camper Cabin C-3

S T A T E   P A R K

Big Woods Loop

Bjorkland Lake

T

Slough Lake

39

31. Lake Maria State Park

Picnic Area

(T) Trailhead

View

N

0   1/4 mile

0   1/4 kilometer

true box turtles live south of Minnesota. Blanding's turtles may travel over a mile to lay their eggs, and a sign along the main park road warns you of a turtle crossing.

Lake Maria State Park is maintained as one of the state's natural, wilderness parks. All of the camping is hike-in. The 1,590-acre park has three camper cabins that sleep six people each. The cabins have vault toilets and wood stoves but no electricity or running water. Other facilities include 17 backpack campsites, two primitive group camps, a picnic area, and rowboat and canoe rentals. Cross-country ski trails are groomed in winter. Contact the park at 763-878-2325.

How to Get There

From Minneapolis–St. Paul, head north about 35 miles on I-94 to Monticello. Exit on MN 25 east. The route to the park is somewhat complicated but well marked with signs. Turn left on West Sixth Street in Monticello. Take a right on Elm Street to Wright County 39, where you head west, a left turn. Drive about 7 miles to Wright County 111 and turn north, to your right. The park entrance is 0.8 mile up the road on the west side.

The Trail

Drive past the park office and turn left on the road to the trail center and horseback riders'

Deciduous Forests

Prairie leading to the Big Woods

parking areas. There are two parking areas at the trail center, which has some interpretive displays. The trail starts on the south side, between the parking lots. Turn left onto the Big Woods Trail, a wide dirt path. Continue past the horseback parking area, on your left. Another trail angles in from the right, but continue straight ahead. You descend slightly and walk into an open area.

The trail makes a 90-degree left turn. Another trail intersects from the left. Stay straight ahead and ascend slightly above a marsh to your left. Cross the park road, just east of the information office.

Now the trail goes through an open field. Blooming wild bergamot and purple aster were common during a mid-August hike. Soon you pass into an area of young maple. At the next intersection, turn right to Anderson Hill, the park's highest point. A bench sits at the top of the lookout, offering a view of farmland to the east and the park's forested hills to the southeast.

At the bottom of Anderson Hill, you head back into the woods on a packed-dirt trail. This is the Big Woods. The smell of basswood blooming was everywhere in the park, but the fragrance was particularly noticeable through this trail section.

Pass by spur trails to backpack campsites B-1 and B-2. They're marked with signs. At the next Y-intersection, marked with a sign, bear right on the Big Woods Trail. Pass the trails to campsite B-3, then the one to camper cabin C-1. To your left is an area of downed trees that have been cut to allow trail access.

Pass a trail that leads to the left and continue straight ahead. Soon you walk between marshes on either side. The trail ascends slightly, and the spur to campsite B-4 goes off to the left, down to a small lake. At a T-intersection, turn right in an open area to the park's namesake Lake Maria, 0.5 mile to the west. There's a boat ramp and picnic area with a toilet and water here.

Walk the trail back to its intersection with the Big Woods Trail. Turn right and pass the spur to campsite B-5. To the left is camper cabin C-2. The trail bisects the marshy lake. Butter-and-eggs were blooming here.

The hiking trail meets a park road. There's a small parking spot here. Turn right and follow the road about 0.2 mile as it curves along the southern end of the small lake. This park road meets the main road to Lake Maria at a T-intersection. Head right for about 50 paces, then pick up the trail on your left. A slight ascent takes you to another T-intersection, where you turn left onto the Kettle-Kame Trail. Kettles and kames are depressions and hills left by glaciers, so as you might expect the trail ascends and descends through this section. The mixed basswood, maple, and oak woods still surround you.

Curve around a small pond on your right and a marsh on your left. Pass the spur trail to camper cabin C-3 to your right. The trail makes a hairpin turn left. At the next three-way intersection, stay right and follow the Kettle-Kame Trail a little more than 0.1 mile to the trail center. A doe and fawn were browsing in the woods near where we finished this hike.

32

Minnesota Valley National Wildlife Refuge, Louisville Swamp Unit

Total distance: 9.3 miles

Approximate hiking time: 4.5 hours

Difficulty: Easy

Vertical rise: Minimal

Maps: USGS 7½' Jordan East and Jordan West quads, Minnesota Valley National Wildlife Refuge map

The national wildlife refuge system was born in 1903 when President Teddy Roosevelt ordered a small mangrove-covered island in Florida preserved for native birds. Today more than 500 refuges are located in all 50 states.

The Minnesota River valley refuge runs from Fort Snelling in St. Paul to Jordan, south of the metropolitan area. Its information and visitor center is located in Bloomington, south of the Minneapolis–St. Paul International Airport. Information about refuge activities and maps is available. The center also houses exhibits on habitat and wildlife. From I-494, drive south on 34th Avenue. Turn east on East 80th Street. The entrance is about 0.25 mile on the right-hand side of the road. The telephone number is 952-854-5900.

The Louisville Swamp Unit, south of Shakopee, is one of eight management areas and contains 2,600 acres. It takes its name from the township, which is named for Louisville, Kentucky, a settler's previous home. Louisville Swamp contains a variety of habitats. There are prairie remnants, oak savanna, floodplain forest, and old fields. The remains of two farmsteads can be seen along the trails.

The swamp is a wetland that sits just east of the Minnesota River. The much larger Glacial River Warren drained Glacial Lake Agassiz about 10,000 years ago. Warren "was a high-volume stream competent enough to erode a deep trench across the entire state," according to a history of the state's geology. Once the giant lake began

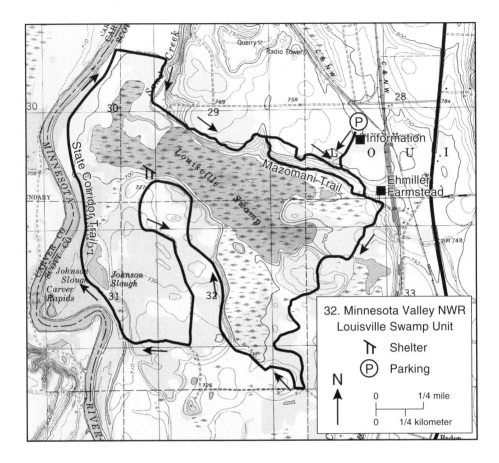

to drain away, the ancient river became a mere trickle, in relative terms. What the early settlers called prairies are remnants of the ancient river's channel bottoms.

Today, the lower Minnesota River valley spreads out in marshes, ponds, and wet woodlands. Natural scientists try to educate people about the value of wetlands, which act as filters for surrounding land. Wetlands also provide habitat for birds and other animals, particularly beavers, muskrats, and mink. Apparently Louisville Swamp is beaver heaven. These large, active rodents have dammed enough water to kill hundreds of acres of trees and flood private property and roads. The refuge staff tries to manage the animal population, but admits the beavers are winning.

How to Get There

From Minneapolis, head south on MN 169 past Shakopee. Look for the large, brown Minnesota Valley National Wildlife Refuge, Louisville Swamp sign. Turn west on 145th Street. Just past the railroad tracks is a large parking area on your left.

The Trail

Find the trail just behind three large, covered signs that include a map of the trail system.

Deciduous Forests

The Ehmiller farmstead

Head south on the Mazomani Trail, and pass by the Little Prairie Loop on your right. An overlook, with a bench, gives a good view of Louisville Swamp. At the next intersection, stay to the left and continue through oak savanna. Acorns crunched under our feet during a fall hike.

Descend the ridge to the old Ehmiller farmstead. Part of one building remains, and shrubs and vines grow over the low walls and through window openings. Another building has more walls and part of its roof. Sumac has grown up around the buildings.

Continue into the bottomland area of tall cottonwood on a wide, packed-dirt path. Downed tree limbs litter the bare ground. About 0.5 mile past the old farm site, cross a bridge over tree-lined Sand Creek, which flows into the swamp. The next part of the trail has some hills and sandstone outcrops.

Bicyclists also use this trail, and one guy whizzed past us. We wondered if we'd see him sprawled farther down the trail after encountering some rocks.

Cross another bridge over the creek, and turn right onto a road that provides access to the swamp. A large boulder deposited by a glacier sits to your right. Make another right turn onto the trail in a few hundred feet. Next, the trail follows the ridge along the swamp. About 1.5 miles past the boulder is a T-intersection. Just to the right is the Jabs farmstead, with crumbling stone buildings and a small hut, at the southern edge of the swamp. A sign gives information about the family of dairy farmers who lived here about 1905. Tall, dead trees stick up from the floodplain to the north.

Head back to the intersection and continue straight ahead, past a shelter. Pass a trail on your right that loops southwest toward Johnson Slough, then rejoins the main trail about 0.5 mile farther. Pass this intersection and follow the trail as it curves to the right in an open area with a shelter, picnic table, and fire pit. A hand pump also provides drinking water.

Pass an intersection where the State Corridor Trail continues upriver, to your left. The trail passes through oak savanna as it heads to the bank where the Minnesota River makes an oxbow curve. Just north of the curve is a campsite with a fire pit and picnic table, on your left. To your right is Johnson Slough.

Continue straight ahead as the trail again comes near the river, which is lined with large cottonwood, ash, willow, and some maple. The trail curves to your right, away from and then back toward the river. For the next mile, the trail follows the river, although trees obscure the view much of the way. This section also can be wet and muddy.

The trail makes a 90-degree right turn and crosses Sand Creek in a little less than 0.5 mile. Turn right at the next intersection, where the State Corridor Trail heads north, to your left. Continue straight ahead until you meet another access road. Turn right and descend toward the northern edge of the swamp through cottonwood and sumac.

Meet an intersection with the Mazomani Trail Loop and turn left. The ridge here, covered in oak and blooming goldenrod when we hiked, used to be a riverbank. Turn left at the next intersection, which is just above the Ehmiller farm site. You're back on the section of trail leading to the parking area.

33

Nerstrand Big Woods State Park

Total distance: 3.2 miles

Approximate hiking time: 1 hour, 45 minutes

Difficulty: Easy

Vertical rise: 150 feet

Maps: USGS 7½' Nerstrand quad, Minnesota Department of Natural Resources state park map

This is the Big Woods of Laura Ingalls Wilder fame. Even though Laura's Big Woods were in Wisconsin, it was the same type of dense maple, basswood, elm, ironwood, and green ash forest. French explorers called the area—running northwest to southeast through Minnesota's midsection—*Grand Bois* or *Bois Fort*. Pioneers picked up the name in English, and it stuck.

The settlers also picked up their axes. They began cutting down 5- to 10-acre lots for firewood. When machines made logging easier, major clear-cutting was done on several hundred park acres. Statewide, the Big Woods provided lumber for houses and bridges, fuel, fence posts, and barrel staves. Today, only a small portion of the original 5,000 square miles of the Big Woods remains.

The park also is named for the town of Nerstrand, 2 miles east. A railway village incorporated in 1878, the town was named for a founder's home in Norway.

Platteville limestone that formed on the bed of a shallow sea about 500 million years ago underlies the park's rolling hills and valleys. This was a peaceful geologic period, compared to the much older era of volcanoes that formed Minnesota's North Shore. The land was low-lying and covered with vegetation, and ancient mollusks swam in the shallow ocean.

About 150 feet of clay glacial drift covers this bedrock throughout most of the park. Glacial meltwater rushed through what now is the Prairie Creek watershed, eroding a

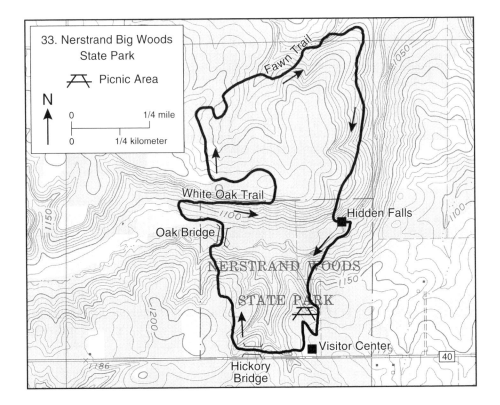

33. Nerstrand Big Woods State Park

🏕 Picnic Area

N

0   1/4 mile

0   1/4 kilometer

Fawn Trail

White Oak Trail

Oak Bridge

Hidden Falls

NERSTRAND WOODS

STATE PARK

Visitor Center

Hickory Bridge

40

deep valley and exposing the limestone there and at the rock shelf of Hidden Falls.

The shaded forest makes this a great park for spring wildflowers that prefer cool, moist conditions, like trillium, bloodroot, and Jack-in-the-pulpit. The park is part of a small area where the rare dwarf trout lily can be found.

The park has a campground with 51 semimodern sites, 27 of which have electricity, showers, and flush toilets. There are four rustic walk-in campsites, a group camp, picnic areas, and a trailer sanitation station. Contact the park by calling 507-334-8848.

How to Get There

From Northfield, which is about 35 miles south of Minneapolis–St. Paul, head southeast on MN 246 for 11 miles. The road jogs south, then meets Rice County 40. Turn west and drive 2 miles to the park entrance.

The Trail

Head past the visitor center and park in the picnic area lot. The trail begins at the southeast corner of the lot and heads south past the visitor center. Just before Rice County 40, the trail turns right. Pass over Hickory Bridge and turn right onto the trail that enters the woods. At the next intersection, turn left. Turn right onto the Fern Hill Trail at an intersection with the group camp trail, to your left. There is a Hiking Club Trail sign here.

This section of trail descends slightly through an area with more grasses. The trail curves right, then 90 degrees left at Oak Bridge over Prairie Creek. Just past the bridge is a T-intersection. Turn left onto

Deciduous Forests

White Oak Trail. For the next 0.6 mile the trail ascends the side of a hill. Here the Big Woods contains some oak.

At a Y-intersection, turn left onto the Fawn Trail. Here the trail, which has some root-covered spots, goes up and down small hills. The trees are more widely spaced here, but their canopies merge to form a leafy roof. A single shaft of sunlight lit a maple leaf, seemingly suspended in midair as it hung on a spider thread.

In about 0.5 mile you come to an intersection where the Fawn Trail heads right and the straight-ahead path meets the Hope Trail loop. Turn right. Torrential rainfall in 1998 washed out banks along ravines and created deep gullies. Trail rehabilitation has started, and park staff estimate that the work will be completed by December 2005.

This section of the Fawn Trail is designated "more difficult" and continues in ascents and descents along ravines. In about 0.6 mile, the trail makes a hairpin turn right to follow Prairie Creek southward. The trail continues about 50 feet above the creek. Fences have been erected in this area to keep deer from eating the forest understory. Lots of wood nettle, a plant with stinging fibers, grows here. Pass the intersection with the White Oak Trail, which angles in from the right.

At the next intersection, follow the sign left to Hidden Falls. Cross the creek. Turn left and head down steps to a viewing area for the falls, which were completely dry when we hiked. Continue straight ahead from the steps to a boardwalk over a "sensitive area," where the dwarf trout lilies grow. In the spring, marsh marigolds, wild ginger, hepatica, trillium, and bloodroot grow on the moist forest floor.

Ascend about 26 wood and gravel steps separated with wide landings. A moderate incline on a crushed rock path takes you back to the picnic area parking lot.

34

Sibley State Park

Total distance: 5 miles

Approximate hiking time: 2.5 hours

Difficulty: Moderate with a steep climb to Mount Tom

Vertical rise: 185 feet

Maps: USGS 7½' Mount Tom quad, Minnesota Department of Natural Resources state park map

The woods of Kandiyohi County were said to be the favorite hunting grounds of Minnesota's first governor, Henry Hastings Sibley. Deciduous hardwoods covered rolling hills where deer browsed, and marshes surrounded small lakes filled with waterfowl. Later, other area residents appreciated the area's geologic features—the glacial Alexandria moraine of rocks, sand, and gravel deposited 10,000 years ago. The glacial debris, or drift, left in Sibley State Park measures as deep as 450 feet, making it some of the deepest in the state. Mount Tom, at 1,375 feet, is the tallest point for 50 miles.

Glaciers also formed the 194 lakes in Kandiyohi County. In some cases, huge chunks of ice were trapped in glacial till, or debris. This left steep-sided lakes filled with meltwater. Other lakes formed as glaciers gouged depressions in the land.

The county's name is taken from a Dakota phrase that means "where the buffalo fish come." Historical accounts note that buffalo fish used to spawn, "sometimes in immense numbers," in the area's lakes.

These lakes also affected the area's vegetation. The park sits on the border of Minnesota's prairie and deciduous forest. To the west, periodic fires renewed the prairie and prevented forests from taking hold. However, the abundant lakes somewhat protected the park area from fire, and oak savanna became a common habitat. Ironwood, basswood, hackberry, green ash, and aspen also grow on the hills and ridges.

Mount Tom has attracted humans for hundreds of years. Stone pipe fragments have been found, suggesting that the point may

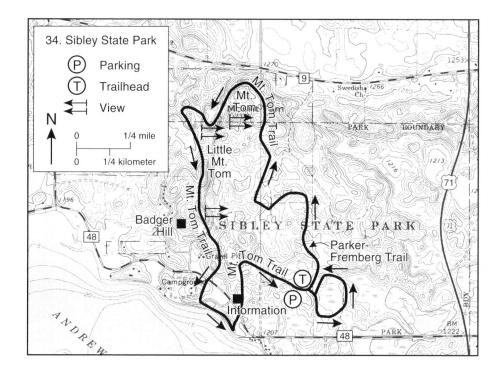

have had significance to native people. Local residents suggested forming a state park near Mount Tom in 1916, and the state legislature appropriated $25,000 to buy land three years later. The county ran the park until 1931. Veterans Conservation Corps members built roads, trails, campgrounds, and buildings from 1934 to 1937.

Today, the park has 134 semimodern campsites, 53 with electricity, three primitive group camps, a horseback riders' camp, a picnic area, and an interpretive center. Boats and canoes can be rented for use on Lake Andrew. A trailer sanitation station with flush toilets and showers is available. The park's phone number is 320-354-2055.

How to Get There

The main park entrance is 15 miles north of Willmar off US 71. Turn west on MN 48 and drive 1 mile to the information office.

The Trail

Just past the information office, turn right and drive to the interpretive center parking lot. This park has excellent displays and brochures and a very knowledgeable staff.

Start the Pondview Trail at the east end of the parking area. At an intersection with a mapboard, go straight ahead through a small area of oak savanna. A sign tells you that oak savanna used to account for about 5.5 million acres of Minnesota's Mississippi River bluffs and deciduous forest but that only 4,400 acres remain. Pass an unmarked intersection to your left and continue straight ahead on the gravel path.

Pass through a grassy area where goldenrod, purple aster, gray-headed coneflower, hoary vervain, blazing star, wild bergamot, sunflowers, black-eyed Susan, and thistles were blooming in August. Lots of turkey-foot grass also was growing here.

The trail curves left around a pond surrounded by sedges and cattails. About halfway around is a wooden bridge with a viewing area. A few steps farther along is a bench overlooking the pond. Cedar trees grow here and there among the grasses and shrubs.

Continue around the pond and stay to the left as you circle back to the oak savanna. At the unmarked intersection, or the one with the mapboard, turn right. You'll end up in the same place. The actual trails don't correspond to those on the park's summer trails map on this side of the Mount Tom road. However, the trails are easy to see, and you should be able to follow this description.

Pass a bench off to your right, and follow the trail as it bears left and goes up and down a small hill. At a T-intersection, turn right. You should see a "deer exclosure" sign marking a trail to your left.

At the next two mapboards, go straight ahead. The wide mowed trail goes up and down the small glacial hills, through oak and prairie restoration areas to your right. In about 0.4 mile you come close to the campground, and we could see a few tents through the trees to the left. A large area of aspen grows on a hill to your right where the trail makes a sharp left. A narrow, overgrown trail intersects to your right. The brown hiking sign was hidden in shrubs. Turn right. If you meet a paved campground road, go back about 50 steps.

The trail is a narrow footpath here. A sign marked "2" points left; follow this. You come to a four-way intersection in an open area with the campground to your left. Turn right at the brown and yellow wooden Mount Tom sign. The trail descends with timbers widely spaced as steps.

Go straight ahead at an unmarked intersection. The trail ascends with timber steps.

The trees are denser here. Fallen logs covered in thick moss lie on the ground. You're now ascending toward Mount Tom, and the incline is noticeable. The trail emerges into an open grassy area at the top of a steep hill and follows the ridgeline to your left. The silvery leadplant, partial to drier soils, grows here.

A short section of asphalt trail drops steeply, passes a pit toilet, and enters the Mount Tom parking lot. Head up the steep asphalt path to your left, and check out the granite overlook building. Signs give information about the types of trees in the forest below, and Mount Tom's history. Nobody seems to know where the name comes from.

Back in the parking lot, head to your left. Look for Hiking Club and Lake Andrew Trail signs. A steep ascent leads to rock and timber steps up to Little Mount Tom. After checking out this view, head back down the steps and turn left. In about 0.2 mile you meet a gravel park road that heads west, to your right, to Lake 21. Follow the trail sign and turn left for about a hundred steps on the road. Catch the hiking trail to your right.

For the next 0.4 mile, the trail ascends and descends small hills. Unmarked trails also intersect the Mount Tom Trail, so follow the Hiking Club signs. At a four-way intersection, go straight ahead. The right-hand trail heads to the group center. Shortly, you meet a short, steep spur trail to Badger Hill, with a bench and a view of the hills to the southwest. Back at the main trail, turn right. Make a steep descent, above and parallel to the Mount Tom road. The trail continues to descend in switchbacks until you cross a gravel park road.

Head up a hill and stay to your right at the next Hiking Club sign. Cross MN 48 and head to Lake Andrew. One of the area's first settlers named the lake for himself, carving "Lake Andrew" on a big cottonwood along the shore. Just above the shoreline, cross the park road and head left, at a Hiking Club sign, along the Lakeview Trail. The trail rises to about 25 to 30 feet above the shore. Continue straight ahead at an unmarked intersection.

Shortly the trail makes a sharp left, crosses the paved bicycle path, then crosses MN 48. This section heads back into the woods and up and down a small hill. Cross the paved road that goes to the interpretive center. A boardwalk crosses a low area. Turn right at a four-way intersection with a mapboard. Keep right at the next intersection, marked with a Hiking Club sign. The trail enters an open grassy area just west of the interpretive center and its parking area.

35

Whitewater State Park

Total distance: 4.2 miles

Approximate hiking time: 3 hours

Difficulty: Moderate to difficult

Vertical rise: 300 feet

Maps: USGS 7½' Elba quad, Minnesota Department of Natural Resources state park map

This park isn't named for churning rapids but rather for the water's appearance when spring runoff washes light-colored clay deposits into the river. The Dakota name was *mini ska,* "white water." A township and village in next-door Wabasha County use a derivation of this name, Minneiska. The county where Whitewater State Park is located, Winona, also gets its name from the Dakota. Winona was a cousin of the last chief in a long line called Wabasha. Winona was the name given to a family's first-born daughter.

Farther north near Red Wing, the village of Maiden Rock across the Mississippi River in Wisconsin commemorates a story about another Winona. The legend says this young Dakota woman leapt to her death in the river and rocks below rather than marry the young man her parents preferred but whom she didn't love.

Southeastern Minnesota lies beyond the edge of the last glacier that covered the state. However, the region isn't free from glacial effects. Previous glaciers released meltwater streams that carved deep into the sedimentary rock left at the bottom of a 500-million-year-old seabed, creating high ridges separated by flat valley floors. These streams and rivers wind through tortuous bends around ridges on their way to the Mississippi. If you've never left the rolling hills of central Minnesota or the flat prairies of the southwest, this part of the state is a wonderful surprise.

The whitish clay that gives the river its name is part of the fine-textured, stone-free

Deciduous Forests

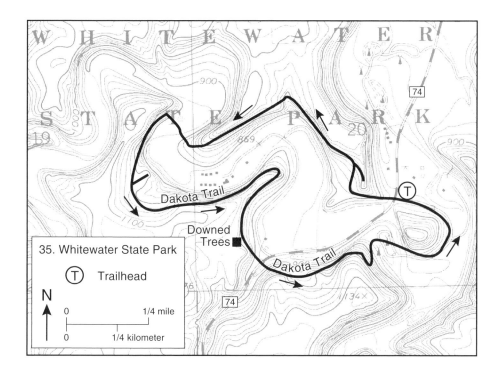

35. Whitewater State Park

(T) Trailhead

N

0   1/4 mile

0   1/4 kilometer

loess, left over from previous glaciers, that blew over the area thousands of years ago. The slippery soil is extremely prone to erosion, something the European settlers found out after they removed the original vegetation for farming and pastures. Deep gullies formed on hillsides, where mud slid down into ravines, clogging streams and rivers. Towns flooded regularly until the settlers gave up and moved on.

Conservation department expert Richard J. Dorer was the driving force behind sweeping measures designed to revive the area. On the steep slopes, grasses, shrubs, and trees were planted. On the high blufftops, contoured fields and terraces were created. Dikes caught runoff, and the state purchased land that was prone to serious erosion. Other land was set aside in wildlife management areas and state parks. Today, a large section of southeastern Minnesota along the Missis-

sippi River valley is recovering as a state forest that commemorates Dorer.

Whitewater State Park is 2,700 acres of limestone bluffs and deep ravines covered in maple, oak, shagbark hickory, and basswood. Brown, rainbow, and brook trout swim in the park's spring-fed namesake river and in Trout Run Creek. The park contains two semimodern campgrounds with 112 sites—47 of which have electricity, showers, and flush toilets. One camper cabin with electricity can be rented, and the park has six walk-in campsites.

Other facilities include a trailer sanitation station, two picnic areas, a nature store, a fishing pier, and a swimming area. A year-round group center, which can accommodate 132 people, has cabins, a dining hall, and a building with showers and flush toilets. A primitive group camp also is available. Contact the park at 507-932-3007.

Stepping-stones across the Whitewater River

How to Get There

Whitewater State Park is located between Rochester and Winona. From Rochester, head east about 18 miles on US 14. Turn north on MN 74 for about 6 miles. From Winona, head north on MN 61, then follow US 14 west for about 18 miles. Turn north on MN 74. In either case, you'll be approaching the park from the south. The park office, if you need to buy a permit, is farther north.

If you're coming from Minneapolis–St. Paul, head down scenic MN 61 about 70 miles, past Wabasha and Kellogg. Turn southwest on MN 74 and continue 17 miles, through Elba, to enter the park from the north.

The Trail

Park at the nature store/gift shop south of the park office on MN 74. Cross the road to the start of the Dakota Trail. This is a Hiking Club route. The trail immediately heads up more than 230 steps to the base of a limestone bluff. It's another hundred-plus steps to the blufftop. The last section of steps is so steep it's like a ladder! Turn right to the Coyote Point overlook, a steep drop-off with no railings.

Head left, back to the main trail. The packed-dirt path has some rocks and roots as it follows the bluff top. A sign on the right indicates Ice Cave Point, but this isn't marked on the park trail map. In about 0.5 mile you come to the intersection with the Coyote Point Trail, which heads right to one of the campgrounds. Stay to your left.

Continue along the top of the bluff, with steep drop-offs in spots, as the trail ascends and descends. Pass an unmarked trail to the right, and continue straight ahead. The path is narrow, studded with small rocks, and goes between larger boulders. Shortly, you come to a stone ledge overlook on your left. Be careful because there are no railings.

About 1 mile from the start of this hike, the trail begins a steep descent to the Whitewater River valley. Pass a trail to your right as you continue to the left and descend through a very steep, rocky area. At the river is a brown and yellow park sign. The Valley Trail turns left, but stay on the Dakota Trail to your right. Large, rectangular blocks of limestone have been set across the river for the trail crossing. Another sign marks the Dakota Trail to the left, where you turn and begin angling up another bluff through an open forest.

At the top is a short spur to Signal Point overlook, which gives a view of the bluffs on either side of the river valley. Return to the main trail, and turn left. This trail section goes along the high blufftop, with the river to your left. Jack-in-the-pulpit, wild ginger, and several kinds of ferns grow in the open forest with some shrubby understory. You pass high above the modern group camp to your left.

In about 0.7 mile, turn right to Eagle Point, another rock ledge with no railing. Back at the sign marking this lookout, a trail heads steeply down the bluff to your right. Stay to the left as the Dakota Trail continues along the blufftop. Descend some stone steps, then through an area of downed trees, some of which were over the trail. The trail becomes very narrow and rocky, as it descends steeply to MN 74.

Cross the road just south of the intersection that heads to the modern group center. The trail ascends through oak, shrubs, ferns, and moss-covered rocks. There are a few more ascents and descents through ravines until you come to a steep descent of more than 100 feet to the grassy south picnic area. Walk to your right to pick up the park road, which winds about 0.5 mile around the base of an isolated bluff to the nature store parking area.

Prairie Grasslands

The Blue Mounds

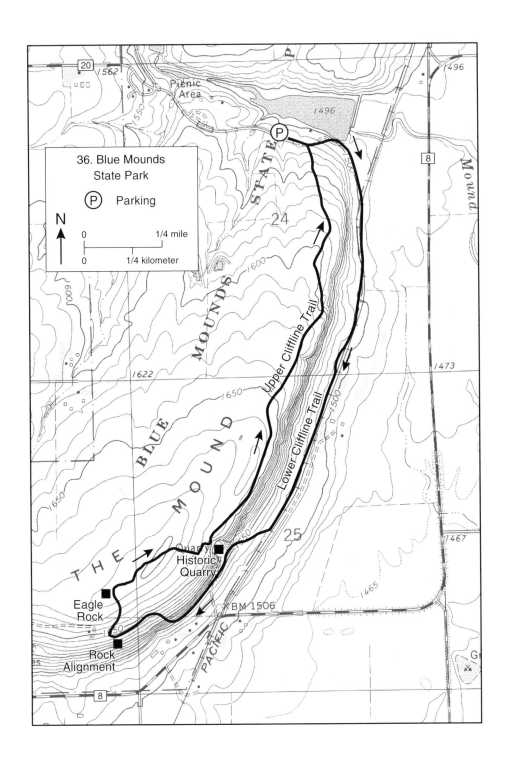

36. Blue Mounds
State Park

Ⓟ Parking

N

0   1/4 mile
0   1/4 kilometer

Upper Cliffline Trail

Lower Cliffline Trail

Picnic
Area

1496

1496

1562

1550

1496

1600

1622

1650

1650

1650

1473

1500

1467

1465

BM 1506

Eagle
Rock

Rock
Alignment

Quarry
Historic
Quarry

BLUE MOUNDS

THE MOUND

STATE P

Mound

PACIFIC

20

8

8

24

25

36

Blue Mounds State Park

Total distance: 4.1 miles

Approximate hiking time: 2 hours

Difficulty: Easy with steep spots

Vertical rise: 234 feet

*Maps: USGS 7½' Luverne quad,
Minnesota Department of Natural
Resources state park map*

Blue Mounds State Park is a tiny bit of the vast tallgrass prairie that once covered the middle United States. In Minnesota, only 1 percent of prairie grasslands remain, according to the Department of Natural Resources.

The park gets its name from a massive outcrop of 1-billion-year-old Sioux quartzite. It's 1.5 miles long and 90 feet high in places. The rock began as quartz sand eroded over millions of years, fell onto an ancient sea floor, and compressed into sandstone. Geologists have noted banding, ripples, and other marks indicating the ebb and flow of tides along many of the park's rocky outcrops. It took more millions of years for weight, heat, and a chemical reaction to turn the sandstone into the very hard quartzite.

Glaciers were the most recent geological event to shape the area. Sioux quartzite underlies much of southwestern Minnesota, supporting some of the high topography that French explorer Joseph Nicollet named the *Coteau des Prairies,* or "Highland of the Prairies."

The park's large outcrop first was called "The Rock." That name appeared on Nicollet's 1843 map of the area and may have come from the Sioux *Inyan Reakah,* or "River of the Rock." Rock County and the Rock River get their names from this geological feature.

In the 1860s and 1870s, settlers heading west began calling the outcrop "The Mound." They noted that in the distance, in dimming light, the cliff appeared blue. The Sioux quartzite itself varies from pink to reddish gray to purple due to iron oxide, but up close

"The Mound" of Sioux quartzite

lichens do make it appear blue in places.

Highly prized for building, the stone was quarried in the park area in the late 1800s, and in nearby Luverne you can see buildings made from the local stone.

The rock outcroppings and shallow soil saved park land from the farmer's plow, but livestock grazing destroyed native grasses and wildflowers and allowed foreign plants to take hold. Since becoming a state park in 1961, the land has been managed to restore native vegetation. Hundreds of wildflowers and grasses grow at Blue Mounds State Park, including prickly pear and brittle cacti. During an August hike, blooming wildflowers included hoary and blue vervain, purple prairie clover, thistle, wild onion, wild bergamot, rough blazing star, western ironweed, Queen Anne's lace, gumweed, goldenrod, red clover, and several varieties of sunflowers and asters. Big bluestem grass grows to 7 feet tall by autumn.

Buffalo were introduced when the land became a state park, and a small bison herd is maintained in an enclosed area. A buffalo roundup and auction occurs whenever the herd gets too large.

The park includes two small lakes, one with a swimming area, created when Mound Creek was dammed in the late 1930s. A drive-in campsite contains 73 semimodern spots—40 with electricity. Fourteen campsites are located in a cart-in area, and a primitive group camp is available. The home of the late Minnesota author Frederick Manfred was donated to the park as an interpretive center, but has been closed for the past several years because of state budget cuts. Contact the park by calling 507-283-1307.

How to Get There

Blue Mounds State Park is 6 miles north of Luverne and I-90, off US 75. Head east on MN 20 for about 1 mile to the park entrance.

The Trail

Continue past the park office about 0.5 mile and park at the Lower Mound Lake picnic and beach area. Look for the brown trail signs with yellow lettering. Head east along the paved biking trail, then on the hiking trail nearer the lake. After 0.2 mile, you'll see the dam to your left, and the Lower Cliffline Trail turns to the right. On your left is farmland, but soon you come to the base of the mound on your right. Fallen boulders lie jumbled at its base, and vertical crevices split its face. The areas are named on the rock climbers' map, and you pass the Receding Ramparts, the Mini Fortress, and are closest to the cliff base at the Prairie Walls.

About 0.6 mile into this hike, a sign points up a crevice in the cliff face for a trail that leads back to the lake as a "One Mile Loop." Stay left on the mowed path that angles slightly away from the cliff.

After 0.9 mile, you join the paved biking trail. On one of our visits, rock climbers were descending the cliff face in this area. At 1.1 miles a trail to the right heads to the Upper Cliffline Trail. Stay straight ahead on the paved bike path until you come to another intersection, with a vault toilet, at about 1.5 miles.

Turn right toward the cliff and head into the shade of the trees that line its base. The narrow dirt trail goes around and between large boulders. A skink darted among the rocks. The trail angles left toward the base of a quarry that was worked from 1919 to 1931. Excavating the rock has left the cliff with a concave amphitheater shape here. The rock walls amplified the cooing of pigeons sitting high up in crevices.

Walk to your left to pick up the trail. A short, steep, rocky ascent brings you close to the top of the mound before the trail angles left and joins the Upper Cliffline Trail. Several unmarked trails also are in the area.

If you've gotten off a main trail, keep going up, and you'll eventually meet the upper trail.

Turn left. This section of trail intersects the Rock Alignment. Boulders of varying sizes run east to west for 1,250 feet. The official park story is that the sun rises and sets in alignment with the rocks on the vernal and autumnal equinoxes, but no one knows who put them there. Many of the smaller rocks are hidden in vegetation, but walk around and you'll notice the line.

Return to the trail, heading south, and in a short distance, you come to the intersection with the Mound Trail. Turn right to Eagle Rock, the highest point in the area. The 360-degree view takes in Iowa and South Dakota. At the next intersection, turn right onto the Upper Mound Trail. After little more than 0.2 mile, a trail to the right leads to the Upper Cliffline Trail and the top of the historic quarry. The view is spectacular from this angle, too. You can walk right to the edge of the cliff, so be careful.

Continue across the top of the mound on the Upper Cliffline Trail through expanses of big bluestem, side-oats grama grass, and numerous wildflowers. The Sioux quartzite is exposed in many places. Bend down and look for prickly pear cactus, which blooms in June, and intricate blue-green lichen. From the quarry, it's a 1.5-mile gentle descent back to the lake parking area. You pass several side trails. Trails to your right are the steep, rocky ones you passed at the base of the cliff. A trail to your left leads farther onto the prairie, and intersects with the Mound Trail that parallels the buffalo enclosure.

Bonus Destination

At Pipestone National Monument, Native Americans have quarried the revered stone for hundreds of years. Early explorers heard of a highland, "a mountain, from which the

---

Indians get a sort of red stone, out of which they hew the bowls of their pipes."

Legends about pipestone's origin differ from tribe to tribe. However, one general belief is that the stone formed from the flesh and blood of Native American ancestors, so it was to be used only for pipes. Because ceremonial smoking is important in Indian culture, ornamental pipes are prized possessions. The relatively soft stone is easy to carve, and the monument's site came to be the preferred source for Plains tribes. The instruments came to be called peace pipes because they were present at treaty ceremonies.

George Catlin, a well-known artist who painted scenes of the area and of Native Americans and their culture, visited the quarry in 1836. He sent a stone sample to a scientist who analyzed its chemical content and named the red stone catlinite.

Although many different tribes quarried and used the pipestone, the Yankton Dakota negotiated a treaty to control the square-mile site in 1858. The federal government came into possession of the site in 1928, and Pipestone National Monument was created in 1937. Only Native Americans can quarry pipestone here.

Quarries run in a north-south line. A circular 1-mile trail passes interesting geological formations, including a waterfall.

Establishing the monument site also preserved a small area of tallgrass prairie, which the trail passes through until it reaches the active pipestone quarries just east of the visitor center. Exhibits on area geology and habitat and Native American culture can be viewed in the center. Native American crafters also demonstrate pipestone carving.

Pipestone National Monument is located in the town of Pipestone. The visitor center and Upper Midwest Cultural Center are open daily, but hours vary. A small admission fee is charged. The phone number is 507-825-5464.

37

Buffalo River State Park

Total distance: 3.3 miles

Approximate hiking time: 1.5 hours

Difficulty: Easy

Vertical rise: Minimal

Maps: USGS 7½' Downer quad, Minnesota Department of Natural Resources state park map

The Buffalo River meanders through what was the bottom of a glacial lake about 9,000 years ago. The massive lake formed as the last glaciers melted, rising and falling to different levels over thousands of years. As it drained away in stages, the lake left a flat plane that makes up northwestern Minnesota. The ancient lakebed also was rimmed with gravel beaches, which can be seen today as long, broad ridges. Part of the Campbell Beach Ridge runs along the state park's eastern edge.

State historians speculate that prehistoric native people used the ridges as ancient highways. Evidence of ancient people has been found about 25 miles southeast of Buffalo River State Park, near Pelican Rapids. Road construction in 1931 unearthed the first human skeleton from North American glacial deposits. Scientists estimate that the skeleton of the teenage girl, dubbed "Minnesota Man" when it was first discovered, dates back anywhere from 5,000 to 1,000 BC.

Buffalo River's name comes from a case of mistaken identity. The Ojibwe called a more southern tributary *pijikiwi zibi*–"buffalo river"–because the great animals spent winters there. When white explorers and settlers came to the area, they started calling the entire waterway the Buffalo River.

Those settlers came looking for farmland, and the soil beneath the thick prairie grasses was deep and fertile. After the Ojibwe gave up this area as part of an 1855 treaty, settlers began moving in. Construction of the Northern Pacific Railroad line that runs

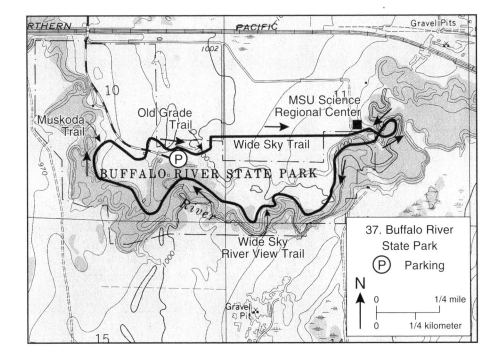

across the park's northern border brought more homesteaders.

However, one of Minnesota's largest remaining areas of prairie remains within the park's borders and in the adjoining state Bluestem Prairie Scientific and Natural Area. Plants found here include rare sticky false asphodel, alkali and slender cordgrass, small white lady's slipper, and scirpiform sedge.

The river itself supports a very different habitat called a riparian or riverine forest. As the river eroded the prairie, it produced a valley wet enough to support cottonwood, basswood, elm, and ash trees. Areas of oak savanna also can be seen between the forest and prairie.

These two habitats attract many different kinds of birds. The higher ridges left over from the glacial lake often are sandy or rocky, so they escaped the farmer's plow and provide "green belts" for migrating

birds. American kestrels, killdeer, mourning doves, northern flickers, belted kingfishers, cedar waxwings, red-eyed vireos, yellow warblers, and western meadowlarks are common in various areas of the park.

Buffalo River State Park was established in 1937 and features a picnic area, a primitive group campsite, a swimming area, and sanitation station for trailers. The campground has 44 sites—35 with electricity—with rest rooms and showers. The park's telephone number is 218-498-2124.

How to Get There

From Moorhead, drive 14 miles east on US 10. Turn south onto the park road.

The Trail

Follow the park road to the campground parking area. Walk back up the road and start on the Old Grade Trail. The trail curves to your right and comes to a Y-intersection. Go left onto the Wide Sky Trail, which is an old asphalt road for a short while. Turn right, following the sign to the Minnesota State University Regional Science Center. You are walking through prairie here. Continue straight as you pass an intersection with the Prairie Smoke Trail to your right. You will see the science center about 0.3 mile across the prairie.

Leave the Wide Sky Trail as it turns right and head to the science center parking lot. Check out the metal prairie grass sculpture and garden, then continue this hike on the science center's Buffalo River Trail, south of the trailhead board. This is an interpretive trail with numbered markers.

Cross an area that changes from prairie to river floodplain to oak savanna. At the Buffalo River, follow the trail loop to your left. Across the river is a high cutbank, where the water erodes the base and the upper part eventually falls. More cutbanks are seen farther along the river.

As you come around the loop, keep the river to your left and continue on a dirt path that goes between markers 4 and 5. Slightly to your left is a bridge over the river, but you want to turn right onto the River View Trail. The trail here is gravel, and you pass behind the Paul P. Feder Observatory that is part of the science center. The observatory's 16-inch telescope is used for public programs, university classes, and research on asteroids.

Turn onto a mowed path to your left. The trail follows the river for about 0.4 mile, then meets the Wide Sky Trail coming in from your right. Continue straight ahead. After about 0.2 mile, you pass the other end of the Prairie Smoke Trail to your right.

The trail follows the river as it bends several times through open prairie, then passes into river woodland. A bench lets you sit and take in the view.

At a Y-intersection, stay to the left and continue past a stone dam. As you pass the

The Buffalo River

Buffalo River State Park

swimming area, walk along the river and pick up the gravel trail at the end of the mowed grass. A removable bridge sat to the right of the trail when we hiked.

Pass through a wooded area with the campground up a small hill to your right. The trail ascends gently. At the far west end of the campground loop road, take the Muskoda Trail to the left. This interpretive trail skirts the woods, with the river farther west, then curves back to the campground and its parking area.

38

Fort Ridgely State Park

Total Distance: 3.9 miles

Approximate hiking time: 2 hours

Difficulty: Moderate

Vertical rise: 160 feet

Maps: USGS 7½' Sleepy Eye NW quad, Minnesota Department of Natural Resources state park map

Fort Ridgely played a crucial role in the US–Dakota War of 1862, repelling two attacks on August 20 and 22 from local Dakota who had repeatedly been misled and cheated by the government. The Dakota gave up all their land except for a strip of land 10 miles either side of the Minnesota River in an 1851 treaty. In exchange, the US government promised money, goods, and services. Many times, the promised annuities arrived late. When they did come, traders often cheated the Dakota, leaving them with little money.

All this frustration came to a boiling point in the summer of 1862. The Civil War had delayed government payments, and the corn crop was poor. Government agents turned many hungry Dakota away from the agency warehouses and denied further credit.

After five young Dakota men killed a group of settlers, tribal leaders, including Chief Little Crow, feared retribution. They decided to go on the offensive and take back their lost lands. The Lower Sioux Agency was the site of the first attack, and 48 soldiers were sent from Fort Ridgely. Half were killed at a ferry crossing below the agency. Chief Little Crow wanted to attack the fort immediately but was overruled. When the Dakota did attack Fort Ridgely several days later, reinforcements had arrived. Two attempts to take the fort failed.

The Dakota were pushed up the Minnesota River and defeated at Wood Lake. More than 500 settlers and an unknown number of Dakota were killed in six weeks of fighting.

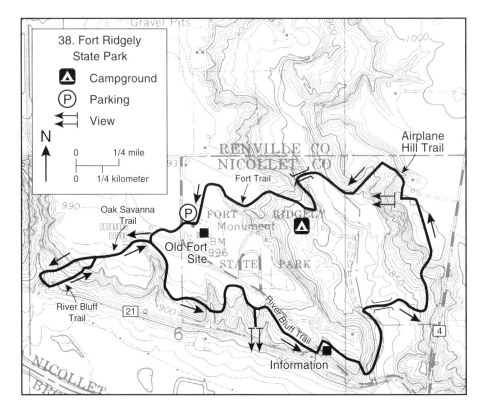

Little Crow and his followers fled to the North Dakota prairie. President Abraham Lincoln commuted the sentences of most Dakota warriors, but 35 were hanged in the largest mass execution ever in the United States, in Mankato in December 1863. The remaining Dakota people were sent to a wet riverbottom camp below Fort Snelling, where many people died. The survivors were moved to reservations out of the state.

Today only the restored stone commissary and wooden powder shed, along with the foundations of soldiers' and officers' quarters, remain in the center of the park. The army formally shut down operations in 1872. The State of Minnesota purchased the fort in 1896 and created Fort Ridgely Memorial Park in 1911.

As was the case in many state parks, the Civilian Conservation Corps developed the facilities here during the 1930s.

Agriculture, logging, and other development have altered the park landscape over the years. Some areas of preserved prairie grass and wildflowers exist near the bluffs overlooking the Minnesota River. The park's oak savannas are small remnants of large groupings of bur oaks along the bluffs. The ravines and hills of the park are covered in ash, basswood, and maple forest.

The 504-acre park has 22 semimodern campsites—13 with electricity—and 17 rustic campsites. Electricity is being added to several more campsites. A horseback riders' camp is also available in the park. A picnic area also contains horseshoe courts, a

The trail to the historic fort site

playing field, and an old amphitheater. Unusual among Minnesota state parks is the nine-hole golf course, built in 1927, set among the wooded hills. The telephone number is 507-426-7840.

How to Get There
Fort Ridgely State Park is 7 miles south of Fairfax on MN 4. Turn west, to your right, on Nicollet County 21. Continue on Nicollet County 30 as it angles off to the right. The park office is just ahead.

The Trail
Continue past the park office to the historic fort site and park there. At the southwest corner of the fort site, cross the road toward the horse camp. Find the trailhead at the south edge of the horse camp parking area. At an intersection with the River Bluff Trail, stay to your right and continue past a small pond. Here the trail passes through remnant oak savanna. Pass a trail to your left, and shortly begin a steep descent to the Min-

nesota River. The trail makes a 90-degree left turn at Brown County 21, then heads back up the steep hillside.

Pass through the oaks again, then stay to your right on the River Bluff Trail. This dirt and mowed-grass portion skirts the golf course, then moves into the forested ravines along the bluffs. There are several steep descents and ascents on this trail section, and you pass under a bridge.

The trail heads through an open area south of the park road. Turn right to an overlook of the river valley. To your right are the ravines where the Dakota warriors came up from the river to attack the fort.

Head back to the main trail and turn right. The trail descends into the trees, then turns left to cross the road. Walk around the park office and pick up the trail on the east side of the road to the campground. Shortly, the trail turns sharply left along the valley of Fort Ridgely Creek. At the next intersection, turn right and shortly cross a bridge over the creek that takes you to the Lower and Upper

Valley trails. Take the trail farthest to the right and head up the hill.

The trail curves left, then the horse trail makes a sharp left turn. Continue straight ahead on the hiking-only path. A moderate ascent leads through grasses to the top of the hill. Walk across the open field. At a Y-intersection, bear left on the Airplane Hill Trail. An overlook gives a view of farmland to the northeast and the Minnesota River valley to the southwest.

The descent from Airplane Hill is short but moderately steep. At a T-intersection, turn left. The next intersection is with the Lower Valley Trail, which heads left and follows the base of the hill. Bear right and return to the bridge next to the park road. Turn right before crossing the bridge and head down to the creek where you can see the kaolin deposits.

Return to the bridge, cross it, and turn left at the Hiking Club sign. Walk along the park road for about 1,000 feet and turn right onto the campground loop road. Pick up the trail off the end of the loop, to the right of the campground toilet.

Another hole of the golf course is to your left, where the trail splits. Continue straight ahead on the Fort Trail. This is an area of thicker ash, basswood, sugar maple, hackberry, and black cherry. Ascend slightly and come out of the woods onto open prairie. The trail turns left and continues to the historic fort site.

39

Glacial Lakes State Park

Total distance: 4.1 miles

Approximate hiking time: 2 hours

Difficulty: Moderate

Vertical rise: 150 feet

Maps: USGS 7½' Starbuck quad, Minnesota Department of Natural Resources state park map

Glacial Lakes State Park is a smorgasbord of landforms left by glaciers that retreated across Minnesota about 10,000 years ago. The park is located in a geological area known as the Leaf Hills that is unique in Minnesota. The name was translated from the Ojibwe for "rustling leaf mountain." This 10- to 19-mile-wide belt of hills runs from Detroit Lakes southeast to Willmar.

The landscape formed after glaciers sheared hills and bluffs down to bedrock. The massive ice sheets dragged this debris along and deposited the rocks, gravel, and dirt elsewhere as glaciers melted. Boulders found in the park contain rock that probably came from northeastern Minnesota and Canada. Some of the state's deepest glacial debris, which geologists call till, can be found in this park.

This is the place to see the kames, kettles, eskers, and moraines typical of glacially sculpted landscapes. Kames are conical hills formed when till flowed into and down holes in the icy mass. Eskers formed when meltwater snaked in streams beneath glaciers, leaving debris in winding ridges. Kettles are depressions formed after breakaway chunks of glacier melted. End moraines are the debris dumped by a glacier's front after it starts melting.

The park also sits at the boundary between western prairie and eastern hardwood forests. Less than 1 percent of the original Minnesota prairie exists, and some is preserved at Glacial Lakes because the hilly terrain was hard to farm. Big and little bluestem grass, side-oats grama grass,

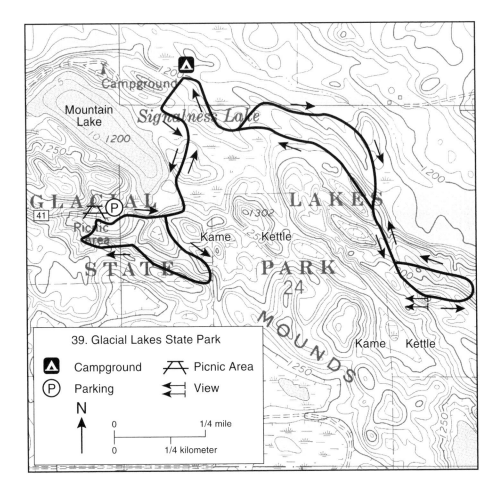

39. Glacial Lakes State Park

🅰	Campground	🛆	Picnic Area
Ⓟ	Parking	⇄	View

N

0 — 1/4 mile
0 — 1/4 kilometer

Indian grass, prairie clover, pasqueflower, coneflowers, goldenrod, lead plant, blazing star, thistles, and prairie onion are some of the prairie plants that grow here. Swamp milkweed, joe-pye weed, and yellow and spotted jewelweed grow in the wetter areas.

Migrating waterfowl and other birds and wildlife take advantage of the park's small lakes, ponds, and marshes. Spring-fed Mountain Lake lies entirely within the park, making it especially clear.

The park has a campground with 39 sites, 14 of which have electricity. A modern shower and toilet building is located in the lower campground. A swimming area, picnic grounds, a horseback riders camp, two group camps, six backpack camping sites, and a boat ramp are available. Contact the park by calling 320-239-2860.

How to Get There

From Starbuck, which is west of Glenwood, head south on MN 29 for 5 miles. Go straight ahead on Pope County 41 as MN 29 heads westward. The park entrance is about 3 miles south.

The Trail

Drive east on the park road past turns to the beach and boat ramp to the left and the horse and group camps to the right. Park in the picnic area lot. The trail, marked with a Hiking Club sign, starts at the east end and begins to ascend immediately. At a Y-intersection, bear left following the Hiking Club sign.

Below on your left is Mountain Lake, which formed when an esker blocked glacial meltwater. Continue straight ahead at the next intersection. The trail begins a moderate ascent into an area of deciduous forest, including American basswood and bur oak. A 2003 storm blew down trees, closing the park for several days.

Cross a boardwalk over a marshy area with lots of arrowhead and jewelweed. The trail ascends to an open area with a bench overlooking the lake. A second boardwalk crosses a marsh with sedges and cattails. Continue past the Council Ring amphitheater and a trail to the lower campground on your left. Stay to your right. Walk through the campground for a very short distance, looking for a large Hiking Club sign at the start of a wide mowed path through aspen, sumac, blazing star, and evening primrose.

About 0.2 mile past the campground, the trail splits at a Y-intersection with a mapboard. Turn left. For the next 0.8 mile the trail goes through a lower area of waist-high grasses, shrubs, young aspen, and sunflowers. Purple closed gentian was blooming during a late August hike.

A boardwalk crosses a wet area, and the trail makes a moderate incline. Soon you see a long, narrow pond to your left. As you come into an area of oak, you pass by two walk-in campsites. The trail ascends to a T-intersection. Turn left onto a wide mowed path with a shallow dirt ravine running down the middle. In about 0.3 mile is the start of a loop around the park's highest point. We went to the right. Watch for rocks imbedded in the trail here. A steep incline leads to the park's high point, where there's a bench. The vista takes in two small kettle lakes to the south, and kames and kettles to the west.

Head left around the loop, which makes several ups and downs through an oak forest. A slight incline brings you back to the start of the loop, where you turn right and walk the same path back to the campsite intersection. This time continue straight ahead. A Hiking Club sign points to the right, the way you came.

The wide mowed path is lined with baby oak trees, and you walk through the wide open prairie, slightly above the path you hiked on the way out to the high point. On a hike late in the evening, the setting sun burnished the hills golden and filled the valleys with warm purple shadows. Pass by the trail that goes to the lower area and narrow pond.

Retrace your steps past the campground, over the boardwalks, and around the southeast end of Mountain Lake. At the first T-intersection with a mapboard, turn left. The trail traces the valley between two kames—one with prairie to your left, the other an oak forest to your right. Several browsing white-tailed deer darted through the trees.

At the top of the hill, the trail moves to the edge of the forest, and you can see the horse camp area below. After heading back into the forest, the trail intersects with another path to the right. Continue straight ahead. As you walk through the valley between the kames, turn back and look at the intersection of hillside angles. The trail leaves the woods at the large picnic area across from where you parked.

40

Kilen Woods State Park

Total distance: 2 miles

Approximate hiking time: 1 hour, 15 minutes

Difficulty: Easy

Vertical rise: 150 feet

Maps: USGS 7½' Lakefield NE quad, Minnesota Department of Natural Resources state park map

This small park sits along the western border of the Des Moines River. Early explorers named this river after the Dakota village *Moingona* in Iowa, where the waterway flows to the Mississippi and gives the state capitol its name.

Tens of thousands of years before explorers walked here, glaciers sculpted the land. The Des Moines lobe covered western Minnesota and reached its most southern point in central Iowa about 14,000 years ago. The glacier retreated swiftly, in geological terms. In a mere 2,000 years, the ice melted and left low conical hills, a few shallow prairie lakes, and numerous wetlands, most of which were drained for farmland. In the Kilen Woods State Park area of Jackson County, the river valley is narrow and bordered by hills and ravines.

Native Americans hunted bison, elk, and waterfowl along the Des Moines River, perhaps as long as 6,000 years ago. Ancient petroglyphs can be seen 30 miles to the north, near Jeffers.

The first white explorers and trappers came to the area in the 1700s. During his 1838 expedition, French explorer Joseph Nicollet made accurate maps and noted three names for the river, including "Moingonan of the Algonkins."

European settlers moved in after the Dakota agreed in an 1851 treaty to move to a reservation along the Minnesota River to the north. Ten years later, unfulfilled agreements, unpaid annuities, and crop failures pushed the Dakota to a violent attempt to

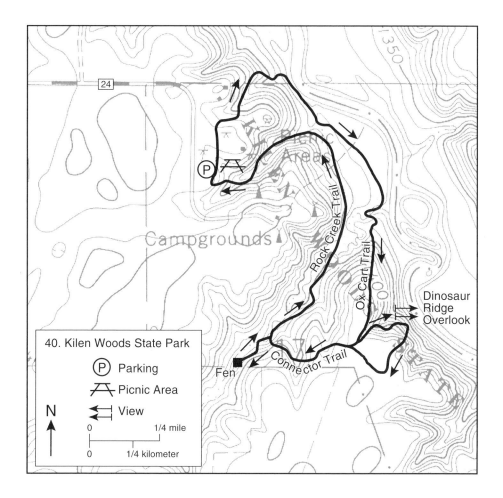

40. Kilen Woods State Park

P Parking

Picnic Area

N

View

0 — 1/4 mile

0 — 1/4 kilometer

Campgrounds

Rock Creek Trail

Ox Cart Trail

Dinosaur Ridge Overlook

Connector Trail

Fen

recapture their ancestral lands. Twenty Jackson Country settlers were killed in the US–Dakota War of 1862. After the war the Dakota were moved out of Minnesota, and settlers returned after several years to turn the prairie into farms.

The 200-acre Kilen Woods State Park packs a lot of diversity into a small area. The river and its vegetation provide a rich habitat for beavers, muskrats, wood ducks, herons, kingfishers, and deer. Oaks grow along the ravines and river slopes. Farther from the banks, rolling hills of big bluestem, little bluestem, side-oats grama, and Indian grass are dotted with wild plums, hawthorns, butterfly milkweed, blazing star, and purple and gray-headed coneflowers. Red admiral and swallowtail butterflies feed off the wildflowers. Oak savannas–areas of large bur oak trees scattered among prairie plants and shrub thickets–cover the park hills higher up from the river. Oak savannas typically are found on slopes and on the downwind sides of lakes and wetlands.

Located entirely within the park is the Prairie Bush Clover Scientific and Natural

The Des Moines River, Kilen Woods State Park

Area. This is one of the world's largest populations of this threatened plant, which has slender, silvery leaflets and pink to creamy-white, open clusters of flowers that bloom in midsummer. A calcareous fen, an area where a constant supply of groundwater charged with minerals prevents complete decay of plant materials, also occurs in the park.

The state park was created in 1945 and named after Agil Kilen, from whom most of the land was purchased. Homestead dugouts, ox-cart trails, log cabin remains, and a pioneer rock bridge can be found within the park boundaries.

Small areas of Class I rapids are on the river. A drive-in campground contains 33 sites, 11 of which have electricity. Four walk-in campsites are located along one of the trails, and two sites give canoe paddlers access to the park. The park's telephone number is 507-662-6258.

How to Get There

From Windom, head south on MN 86, which is joined with MN 60. Drive south on MN 86 about 6 miles. Turn east onto Jackson County 24 and drive about 3.5 miles to the park entrance. Another route is south on MN 71 for 6 miles, west on Jackson County 30 for about 4 miles, then south on Jackson County 17 for about 4 miles to the intersection with Jackson County 24.

The Trail

Park in the lot near the shelter building and picnic area, just south of the entrance. To the left of the building follow the trail signs, including one for the Hiking Club, down an incline with inset timbers along a ravine. The trail meets the Des Moines River and turns to your right. A bridge crosses a stream, which was dry the October day we hiked.

At an intersection with a mapboard, stay to your left toward the river. Walk through a

Prairie Grasslands

meadow of tall grasses right down to the riverbank. The trail turns right, and intersects with the Ox Cart Trail. Turn to your left and cross a bridge over a small stream. Immediately you come to a four-way trail intersection. Continue straight ahead on the Ox Cart Trail through an oak savanna as you start climbing to the Dinosaur Ridge lookout.

The next intersection has a map. Turn left to Dinosaur Ridge, following the Hiking Club sign. As we hiked to the lookout, a huge flock of grackles sat in the trees above us, cawing. They took flight in one swoop of wings and cackling, flying to a group of trees farther downriver.

The Dinosaur Ridge lookout has a wooden platform with a sign giving information on how ice and water shaped the land below. After taking in the view of the peaceful river and its valley, continue on the trail as it curves to your right and goes up and down a ravine. Turn right at the next trail intersection onto what the map calls the "Connector Trail." You pass the Prairie Bush Clover Scientific and Natural Area to your left, and the trail gently descends to a short spur trail to the fen.

Retrace your steps back to the Connector Trail and meet the intersection with the Rock Creek Trail. Continue straight ahead.

At the next intersection, take the trail to the left, which follows a creek ravine and crosses it via a small bridge with handrails. For the next 1,000 feet, the trail ascends moderately to a ridge above a ravine. At a five-way intersection, continue straight ahead on the Rock Creek Trail for about 400 feet. Rock Creek Trail turns to your left, then crosses two small wooden bridges without handrails. The trail makes another moderate ascent to follow the top of a creek ravine and wind back to the building parking area.

Bonus Destination

Thousands of ancient rock carvings mark the Sioux quartzite bedrock that lies on the prairie surface at Jeffers Petroglyphs Historic Site. In the visitor center, a multimedia presentation and exhibits explain Native American culture, prairie ecology, and the petroglyphs. The site is sacred to Native Americans, who conduct religious ceremonies and prayers here.

A 0.75-mile loop trail leads through native and restored prairie. Interpretive signs give information about the plants, including whorled milkweed, prairie thistle, and sawtoothed sage. A boardwalk has been built over the bedrock, where you can see carvings of buffalo, turtles, thunderbirds, and human figures estimated to be more than 5,000 years old.

Another short trail leads to a Sioux quartzite outcrop that was burnished by buffalo and is appropriately called the Buffalo Rub.

Admission is charged to the site, which is open May through September. The Jeffers petroglyphs are about 15 miles north of Windom. From US 71, go east 3 miles on Cottonwood County 10. Turn south on CR 2 and drive 1 mile to the entrance.

41

Lac qui Parle State Park

Total distance: 3.2 miles

Approximate hiking time: 1 hour, 40 minutes

Difficulty: Easy

Vertical rise: None

Maps: USGS 7½' Milan quad, Minnesota Department of Natural Resources state park map

The poetic French name of this state park, lake, and county means "the lake that talks." French explorers translated the Dakota *mde*, or lake and *iye*, or speaks. One traditional story says that the Dakota heard voices coming from the lake. Another tells of sounds echoing along its shores. A third story cites the creaking and groaning of the frozen waters in winter. Still another claims that when the wind was coming from a certain direction, waves would hit stones on shore with a musical sound. A modern traveler's guide says: "The name was most likely given because of the sound of thousands of waterfowl and shorebirds that inhabit this area in the spring and fall."

The lake actually is a wide spot in the Minnesota River caused by sediment flowing in from the Lac qui Parle River. The Minnesota River is a leftover of Glacial River Warren, which drained 10,000-year-old Glacial Lake Agassiz, the largest lake ever to cover the earth. The glacial river carried a lot of water, powerful enough to carve a trench across the state from west to east. A series of small river lakes formed where tributaries dumped sediment in natural dams.

Native Americans hunted the game that lived in the rich river valley. Wahpeton Dakota lived in a village along the lake. Explorers, traders, and trappers also came for the animal resources. Joseph Renville (1779–1846), a French-Indian voyageur well known in Minnesota history, built a trading post enclosed by a stockade at the foot of the lake in 1826. Renville invited mission-

Prairie Grasslands

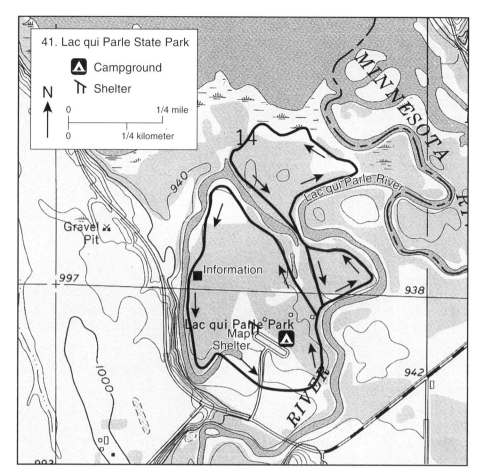

41. Lac qui Parle State Park

🔺 Campground

🏕 Shelter

N

0   1/4 mile

0   1/4 kilometer

aries to his little community in 1835, and the first church in the state was started here. One missionary later translated the Dakota language into a written form and translated the Bible into Dakota. The Minnesota Historical Society maintains a recreated Lac qui Parle Mission site on the east side of the lake, across from the state park.

This wide spot in the river is a haven for waterfowl. In early March, thousands of Canada geese arrive from a wintering spot in Missouri. Swans fly by in April, and pelicans nest on a large island. The park is bounded on the north and west by the Lac qui Parle Wildlife Management Area.

A new campground, with 37 electrical sites, opened at Lac qui Parle State Park in September 2004. A trailer sanitation station also is available. A group camp, horseback riders camp, walk-in campsites, picnic area, swimming beach, and canoe and motorboat ramps also are located in the park. The telephone number is 320-734-4451.

How to Get There

From Montevideo, drive 12 miles northwest on US 59. Head west on Chippewa County 13, which becomes Lac qui Parle County 33, for 5 miles. The park entrance is on the east side of the road.

Floodplain in Lac qui Parle State Park

The Trail

Park at the boat landing on the Lac qui Parle River. Before starting the hike, check out the large relief map housed under an open-sided shelter in the large, grassy open area northeast of the boat landing.

Pick up the trail on the east side of the large, open area, where you will also see a picnic shelter. The wide mowed trail starts to your right along the Lac qui Parle River. Almost immediately, the trail forks. Stay to your right. Blue vervain, American bellflower, thistle, and common burdock were found during an August hike.

In about 0.4 mile is an intersection of four trails at a bend in the Lac qui Parle River, to your right. The trail starts a curvy loop along the Lac qui Parle to where it meets the Minnesota River. Stay on the trail farthest to the right. The river and trail curve and head east, to the right, for about 0.2 mile. The river continues east to meet the Minnesota River, but the trail curves to your left. Here you are walking through the floodplain on the southern end of the lake. Dead trees stud the wide plain of grass and marsh plants that meets the open water.

The trail curves to the left and follows alongside a large oxbow lake, which park staff call "the backwater." Now you're back at the start of the loop. Stay to the right until you come to the next intersection, then turn right again to the open picnic area. You've reversed direction and soon will be walking along the other side of the backwater.

The trail makes a nearly 90-degree curve to the left. Continue straight ahead at an intersection with a sign marking a deer browsing area.

Cross the park road and continue walking along the wide mowed path for about 0.5 mile. After another hairpin curve left, cross a land bridge at the trail to the group camp, to your right.

Cross a park road to the horseback camp and continue walking through an open field. To your left are walk-in campsites. The trail turns left and crosses the park road just above the boat landing.

42

Lower Sioux Agency Historic Site

Total Distance: 2 miles

Approximate hiking time: 1 hour

Difficulty: Steep trail to river

Vertical rise: 200 feet

Maps: USGS 7½' Morton quad, Minnesota Historical Society site map

The Lower Sioux Agency, which sits on a bluff 200 feet above the Minnesota River, was the site of the first attack in the US–Dakota War of 1862. Years of bitterness over 1851 treaties that moved the Dakota to a strip of land 10 miles either side of the Minnesota River collided with late government payments and crop failure to spark the conflict.

The summer of 1862 was a poor year for crops. Dakota living in the riverside reservation were hungry and had been waiting weeks for their annual payments, delayed due to the Civil War. Government agents had turned many Dakota away from the warehouses and denied further credit.

After five young Dakota men killed a group of settlers, tribal leaders, including Chief Little Crow, feared retribution. They decided to go on the offensive, and the agency's traders and stores were the first targets. The Dakota killed all the people who didn't escape and took food and other supplies. Half of the 48 soldiers sent from nearby Fort Ridgely were killed at a ferry crossing below the agency. Chief Little Crow thought it would be smart to attack the fort immediately but was overruled by warriors who headed to the German river town of New Ulm. By the time the Dakota did attack Fort Ridgely, reinforcements had arrived. Two attempts to take the fort failed.

In six weeks of fighting, more than 500 settlers and an unknown number of Dakota were killed. Little Crow and his followers fled to the North Dakota prairie. More than 300 Dakota men were jailed and sentenced to death, but President Abraham Lincoln commuted the sentences of all but 35. There were hanged

Prairie Grasslands

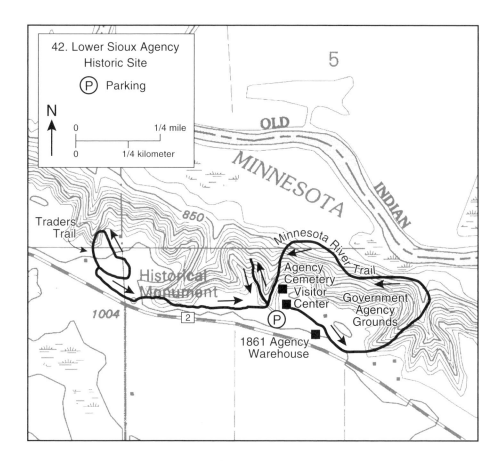

42. Lower Sioux Agency
Historic Site

(P) Parking

N

0   1/4 mile

0   1/4 kilometer

5

OLD

MINNESOTA

INDIAN

850

Traders
Trail

Minnesota River Trail

Historical
Monument

Agency
Cemetery
Visitor
Center

Government
Agency
Grounds

1004

2

(P)

1861 Agency
Warehouse

in the largest US mass execution ever, in Mankato in December 1863. The remaining Dakota people were sent to Fort Snelling, where they lived in a camp along the wet river-bottom. Hundreds of people died, and the survivors were moved out of the state. The government sold the reservation land along the river to settlers, but Dakota people began returning to their homes within a few years. A new Dakota community was established in the 1880s, and today the Lower Sioux Community borders the historic site. A stone warehouse has been restored, and a visitor center has impressive exhibits on Dakota culture and the conflict.

Due to budget cutbacks, the Minnesota Historical Society has closed the interpre-

tive-visitor center. The trails still are open on a limited basis. Contact the agency at 507-697-6321.

How to Get There

From Redwood Falls, head east on US 71 for about 5 miles. Continue southeast on Redwood County 2 when it separates from US 71. The historic agency site is about 2 miles farther on the north side of the road.

The Trail

Parking is available west of the visitor center. The Agency Trail begins on the east side of the visitor center. This straight leg of trail passes between gardens with plants from the time of the US–Dakota War. Pass the

The Minnesota River near a historic ferry site

restored stone warehouse on the original path of the old road between the agency and New Ulm, about 30 miles to the southeast.

Past the warehouse, Agency Trail turns left to loop back to the visitor center. Go straight ahead on the Minnesota River Trail. The trail begins a steep decline through thick forest with ravines on either side at times. At the base of the bluff, a trail leads to the old agency's ferry crossing on the riverbank.

Back on the main trail, cross a wooden bridge over the ravine. Stop to look at two enormous cottonwoods on either side. The trail follows the river, then curves left. It had rained recently, and this lower section of trail was quite muddy.

Now, the trail heads back up the nearly 200-foot bluff to an intersection with the Trader's Trail. Another trail to your right leads to a bench on the bluff line. However, shrubs obscure a river view.

The Trader's Trail starts on the former route to the Yellow Medicine or Upper Sioux Agency. Today it goes through an open grass field, curving right to the start of a small loop. This loop skirts the blufftop, where fur traders operated on the reservation under government license. They sold tools, blankets, clothing, firearms, cooking utensils, and other supplies. Stores and traders' homes also were located here. Turn right and follow the loop past interpretive signs. Turn left to retrace your steps to the visitor center parking area.

43

Split Rock Creek State Park

Total distance: 2.7 miles

Approximate hiking time: 1 hour, 15 minutes

Difficulty: Easy

Vertical rise: Minimal

Maps: USGS 7½' Pipestone South quad, Minnesota Department of Natural Resources state park map

Split Rock Creek takes its name from the gorges it eroded in the Sioux quartzite near the town of Jasper and farther downstream through South Dakota's spectacular Palisades State Park. The creek lies in the only portion of Minnesota drained by the Missouri River, the *Coteau des Prairies* named by an early French explorer. (The more famous Split Rock River and lighthouse are on Minnesota's North Shore of Lake Superior.)

The Works Progress Administration dammed the meandering little creek running through treeless prairie in 1938. The short-term goal was to provide work for local residents. The long-term goal was to create a recreational area for the region. This corner of the state has only a handful of lakes. Indeed, small Split Rock Lake is the only sizable body of water in Pipestone County. This makes the water a haven for aquatic birds. Migrating ducks, geese, pelicans, and swans use it as a stopover on flights north and south.

Elm and ash trees were planted after the area became a state park, but a small hillside of untouched prairie still exists. In the spring, pasqueflower and prairie smoke bloom. Summer wildflowers include prairie roses, yarrow, and starry campion. Goldenrod, asters, sunflowers, and blazing star present their autumn blooms.

At the park's southwest corner, the Split Rock Bridge, listed on the National Register of Historic Places, spans the creek. The single-span stone arch bridge, constructed of locally quarried bluish-pink Sioux quartzite,

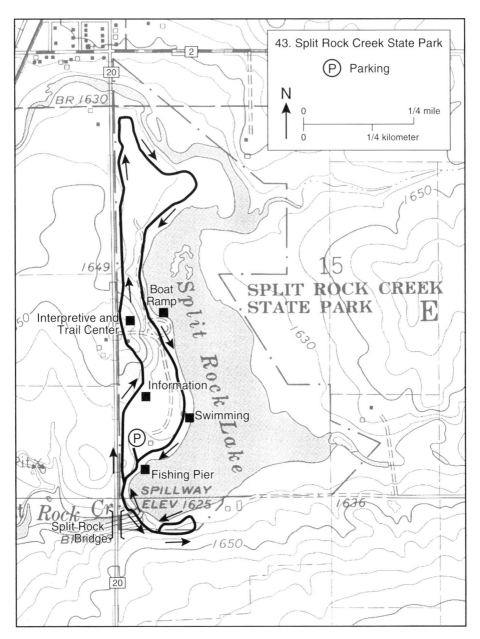

has remained unaltered since its 1938 completion. The bridge's construction "was clearly intended to showcase the area's masonry tradition," according to the Minnesota Historical Society. "The bridge has an almost modernist simplicity, which focuses attention on the natural colors and textures of the local Sioux quartzite."

The park's dam also was built from Sioux quartzite, the same bedrock that forms the

Cattails along Split Rock Lake

massive Blue Mound 15 miles to the southeast.

Split Rock Creek State Park has 34 campsites—17 of which have electricity—a primitive group camp, a swimming beach, a picnic area, a fishing pier, a boat ramp, and a trailer sanitation station. The park's telephone number is 507-348-7908.

How to Get There

From Pipestone, head 6 miles south on MN 23 to Ihlen. Turn left on Judd Street, then right on Pipestone County Road 20, named 50th Avenue on an Ihlen street sign.

The Trail

After passing the information office, turn right and park in the picnic shelter lot. West of the picnic shelter, look for the blue Hiking Club sign. Cross a wooden bridge and follow a dirt path south toward the lake. Pass the fishing pier on your left and continue toward a parking area next to Pipestone County Road 20. The trail curves left to the dam. As you cross the walkway, the historic bridge is to your right. Water trickles down the stacked quartzite blocks, then rejoins the creek as it curves gently and flows under the stone arch.

Across the walkway, the trail turns left and begins a loop. We went to the right. Here the trail enters a wooded area of shrubs and ash and maple trees, one of which is a huge, double-trunked tree. Follow the trail left to the lakeshore, where another large multitrunk maple grows right at the water's edge. When you complete the loop, turn right and cross back over the dam.

Just past the parking area, the wide mowed grass trail divides. Stay to the left and continue past the picnic area's parking road loop, which is on your right. The trail passes through an open area for 500 feet, then crosses the park entrance road. After another 500 feet is a trail intersection with a Hiking Club sign. Stay on the trail to your left.

The trail ascends gently through remnant prairie to a Sioux quartzite building that looks like a watchtower. This used to house an interpretive center. The August day we hiked, butter-and-eggs, goldenrod, lead-plant, and wild bergamot were blooming. This higher vantage point also provides a good view of Split Rock Lake to your right.

The trail ascends gently, and you pass an unmarked trail to the right. Continue straight ahead, passing the campground on your right. The trail comes close to the road several times but is screened by trees in places.

Past the top of the campground loop, the trail continues north for about 1,000 feet and intersects with a short spur trail leading to a bridge over Split Rock Creek north of the lake. The trail curves right and heads southeast, skirting a large open area where park employees have been removing invasive buckthorn. For the next 1,700 feet, the trail basically follows the curve of the creek, although not on the bank. Tall aquatic grasses, young willow, and swamp smartweed, blooming bright pink, grow here.

After passing the group camp to your right, the trail hugs the lakeshore lined with cattails. The trail passes several benches and a dock, then crosses the loop road to the boat ramp. Here the trail gets a bit overgrown with high grasses, and you pass willow and maples. About 1,000 feet past the boat ramp is the swimming beach. Cross it and continue along the lakeshore for another 500 feet to the picnic shelter where this hike started.

44

Upper Sioux Agency State Park

Total Distance: 2.5 miles

Approximate hiking time: 1 hour, 20 minutes

Difficulty: Moderate

Vertical rise: 100 feet

Maps: USGS 7½' Lone Tree Lake quad, Minnesota Department of Natural Resources state park map

Upper Sioux Agency State Park lies around the confluence of the Minnesota and Yellow Medicine Rivers. For hundreds of years, Dakota people inhabited the area, known as "the place where they dig for yellow medicine." To the Dakota, the yellow medicine was the long, slender, bitter yellow roots of the moonseed, also known as yellow sarsaparilla or vine maple.

The US government established the agency, also called the Yellow Medicine, in 1853 to administer terms of an 1851 land cession treaty. The Lower Sioux, or Redwood, Agency was established 30 miles downriver.

Under the terms of the treaty, Dakota land was reduced to a strip 10 miles either side of the Minnesota River from Big Stone Lake near the South Dakota border to Fort Ridgely. In exchange for their land, the Dakota were promised government payments and services. Many times, these payments were late, or were greatly reduced by the deceptive practices of traders. In 1862, annuity payments were delayed several times, and crops planted by the Dakota, who had been persuaded to try farming, were poor.

Bitterness and frustration boiled over after five young Dakota men killed a group of settlers. Tribal leaders, including Chief Little Crow, attacked the Lower Sioux Agency. Most Upper Sioux Dakota didn't participate in the conflict and left the area instead. Both agencies were nearly destroyed, however. The Dakota were defeated after six weeks of fighting in which more than 500 settlers and

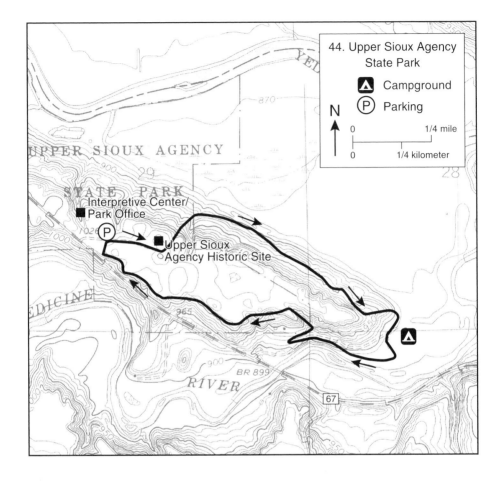

44. Upper Sioux Agency State Park

■ Campground
Ⓟ Parking

N

0   1/4 mile
0   1/4 kilometer

UPPER SIOUX AGENCY
STATE PARK
Interpretive Center/
Park Office
Ⓟ
■ Upper Sioux
Agency Historic Site

RIVER
BR 899
67

an unknown number of native people were killed. After the war, the Dakota people were sent to reservations outside Minnesota. The Dakota population dropped from about 7,000 people before the 1862 war to fewer than 200 in 1870.

The US government returned 746 acres of land to a community group in 1938, and the Upper Sioux Community was established. It is one of the state's federally recognized Dakota communities, along with Prairie Island, Prior Lake, and Morton's Lower Sioux.

Much of the park site is a plateau of glacial drift between the Minnesota and Yellow Medicine Rivers. The lower areas of the park are alluvial, water-carried sediments de-posited by the two rivers. The Minnesota River itself is the ancestor of the much larger Glacial River Warren, which drained Glacial Lake Agassiz, the earth's largest lake ever.

The state park was established in 1963 to protect agency remains and provide recreation for the area. The Minnesota Historical Society has restored an employee residence, the only building remaining from the old agency. Other facilities include a campground with 31 sites—13 of which have electricity. Three walk-in sites also are located off the main campground road, and two tepees can be rented. The park also has a boat ramp and picnic areas. The telephone number is 320-564-4777.

Prairie Grasslands

Rolling prairie trail

How to Get There

From Granite Falls, drive 8 miles southeast on MN 67. The park entrance is on the northeast side of the road.

The Trail

Continue past the park office and interpretive center to the picnic area parking lot. Walk east to the historic agency site. Just east of the buildings and foundations, the trail starts where the trees begin. This is a mixed-use horseback/hiking trail.

The packed-dirt trail immediately begins a steep descent as you head toward the river. Turn right at the first intersection and continue through a mixed hardwood forest. This portion of trail is dense and shady with several gentle ascents and descents. The day we hiked, each step brought scores of frogs hopping out of tall grass along the trail.

In about 0.5 mile, the terrain shifts to prairie. A picnic table marks this point as the trees give way to tall prairie grasses. As the trail heads downhill, you can see the campground with its white tepees to your left. The panoramic view is of the Yellow Medicine River straight ahead and the Minnesota River to your left. The beautiful snow-on-the-mountain was growing near the trail here.

At the base of the hill, turn right and in about 0.1 mile cross the paved park road. The trail continues along the Yellow Medicine River for a little over 0.2 mile, then crosses the road again.

The next section of trail winds uphill steeply, with one switchback curve, through spreading bur oak. We met several horseback riders coming from the opposite direction and had to wait for them to make it down the hill before we could head up.

Snow-on-the-mountain

At the top of the hill, take the trail to the left. Here you skirt the ridge overlooking the Yellow Medicine River valley. The trail goes up and down through small hills. On your right, oaks have grown down the hillsides while prairie grasses fill in the hilltops. Blazing star, goldenrod, butterfly milkweed, blue vervain, and gray-headed coneflower were blooming in August.

Stay to your right as you pass a trail that winds sharply downhill to your left. At the next intersection, a right turn will take you back to the park road and the historic site. We continued straight ahead for another 0.3 mile through the prairie, then turned right to the picnic area parking.

Mississippi River Banks and Bluffs

A Mississippi River vista

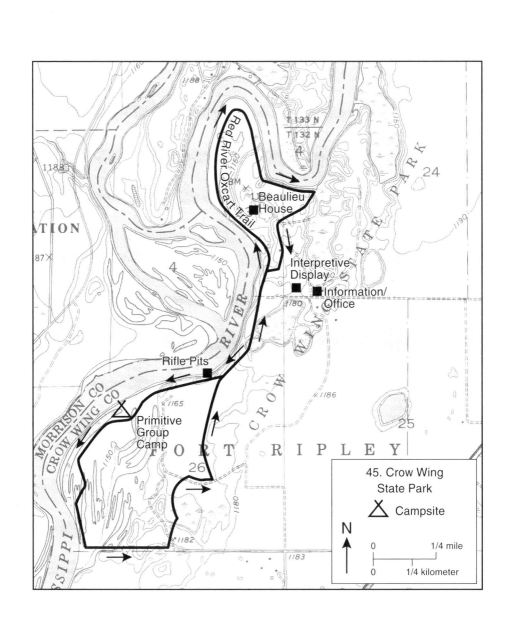

T 133 N
T 132 N
4

Red River Oxcart Trail

Beaulieu
House

Interpretive
Display

Information/
Office

RIVER

Rifle Pits

MORRISON CO
CROW WING CO

Primitive
Group
Camp

FORT RIPLEY

CROW WING STATE PARK

24

25

26

45. Crow Wing
State Park

△ Campsite

N

0   1/4 mile
0   1/4 kilometer

45

Crow Wing State Park

Total distance: 4.9 miles

Approximate hiking time: 2.5 hours

Difficulty: Easy

Vertical rise: Minimal

Maps: USGS 7½' Baxter quad, Minnesota Department of Natural Resources state park map

A lot of history is packed into the area of Crow Wing State Park. Ojibwe lived here as they moved west through the Great Lakes area, fighting with and displacing the Dakota. The area was a major battle site in the long-running hostilities between Dakota and Ojibwe. The river lends its name to the park, county, township, and a historic village, but several versions of how it was named exist. One version says the name comes from the bird-wing shape of the island where the Crow Wing and Mississippi Rivers meet. Another says it's an anglicized version of the Ojibwe word for "raven" or "raven feather." A third explanation links the river's name to the Little Crow line of Dakota chiefs.

The earliest record of a trader near this island is in a list of licenses granted in 1826. Nine years later the Crow Wing post became "the center of Indian trading for all the upper country, the general supply store being located at this place," according to an 1881 report. A branch of the Red River Trail crossed the Mississippi at Crow Wing. Catholic and Episcopal missionaries followed. In 1866, about 600 people lived in the bustling trade town. Then the local Ojibwe were relocated to the White Earth Reservation, and the Northern Pacific Railroad located its Mississippi River crossing in Brainerd, 10 miles north. Bypassed by the railroad, the trading post's heyday was over. Still, for more than 100 years, Crow Wing was the northernmost settlement of Europeans on the Mississippi.

Geologically, the area sits in the far northwestern corner of the Mississippi River Sand

Plains formed by the drainage of a glacial lake. The park area's natural history also includes the intersection of Minnesota's three biomes—prairie, hardwood forest, and pine forest. Climate researchers think the Crow Wing area has seen dynamic shifts between these areas for thousands of years. Original vegetation included oak forests studded with pine and prairie. In low-lying areas, conifer bogs and wet prairies formed. Today, oak, aspen, and jack, red, and white pine fill the park.

Facilities include a semimodern campground with 61 sites, 12 of which have electricity, and showers. One camper cabin without electricity is available. A primitive group campsite includes hand water pumps and toilets, and one canoe campsite is located along the Mississippi. The park rents canoes and boats that can be launched on the Mississippi boat ramp. An enclosed picnic shelter, outdoor picnic areas, and a trailer dump site also are available. The park's telephone number is 218-825-3075.

How to Get There

From Brainerd, go south on US 371—the Great River Road—for 9 miles. Turn west, a right turn, onto Crow Wing County 27. The park information office is 1 mile on the north side of the road.

The Trail

Park in the picnic area lot west of the information office. The Red River Oxcart Trail starts at a covered kiosk, next to a park building that gives information about the park's history. Steps lead down toward the river on this wide asphalt trail that shortly turns to crushed rock. Crow Wing Island is to your left.

Interpretive signs mark historic points along this part of the hike. The trail goes through a wide, flat meadow. Pass a trail to your right and continue straight ahead, through the site of the old trading post and town. Cross a boardwalk. Beaulieu House is to your right. You can walk around the exterior of the house, then head back to the trail.

At a Y-intersection stay to the left, along the river, following the Red River Trail sign. The forest here is an open mix of green ash, aspen, and sumac. The trail is a wide mowed path. About 0.7 mile into this hike, you come to the historic spot where oxcarts crossed the Mississippi River.

As the trail follows a bend in the river, you come to a trail intersection with a Hiking Club sign on the right. Again, stick with the river by heading onto the left-hand path. Continue along the shoreline for about 0.5 mile. At the next intersection, bear left. Here you're walking through a denser mix of basswood and oak. Just past a bench is the historic Episcopal mission site.

Now, the trail ascends slightly to a high area above the boat ramp. From this lookout, Ojibwe kept watch on the river. Walk down the steps to the boat ramp for a good view of the Mississippi.

Climb back up to Chippewa Lookout and head to your left. In about 0.2 mile, you come to a historic trail sign, the site of a one-room schoolhouse. Cross the gravel park road and stay to the left, passing by another trail that leads back to the path you hiked upriver. Shortly you come to the granite Chapel of St. Francis Xavier, on the left. The first Catholic mission in this part of Minnesota was built here, but the building burned down. The stone replacement is a memorial to the historic mission's pastor. Past the chapel, the trail curves right and heads to the interpretive kiosk.

Walk past the kiosk and park building, and continue to the south end of the parking area. Look for a trail entrance marked with an orange diamond, and head toward the river. Pass a trail, marked with a sign, to the Indian Rifle Pits on your left. Go straight ahead to the Red River Trail sign and turn left. The wide mowed path continues along the riverbank for about 0.5 mile. Next comes the primitive group camp, which includes an older log building used for group events.

The trail continues to the right of the group camp parking area, through a large area of milkweed, ferns, young oak, and some pine. About 0.5 mile past the group camp, the trail curves away from the river, then makes a 90-degree left turn at the park's southern boundary. Continue walking through the mixed oak, basswood, and aspen for another 0.2 mile.

Turn left at the next intersection and soon you meet the gravel park road. Turn right and walk along the road for about 0.2 mile, then turn left at the next intersection on a grass trail that leads through the mixed forest again.

Look for a sign leading to the Rifle Pits. This isn't for modern shooters. It's a hilly spot where Ojibwe, who already had gotten guns from Europeans, waited to ambush Dakota warriors, who still were using more primitive weapons. An interpretive sign explains the historic encounter.

Head to your right to hook back up with the Red River Trail, and retrace your steps about 0.4 mile to the parking lot.

46

Fort Snelling State Park

Total distance: 3.6 miles

*Approximate hiking time: 1 hour,
45 minutes*

Difficulty: Easy with a steep climb to fort

Vertical rise: 275 feet

*Maps: USGS 7½' St. Paul West quad,
Minnesota Department of Natural
Resources state park map*

Pike Island in Fort Snelling State Park may be the site of the first raising of a US flag in Minnesota. Lt. Zebulon Pike, of Pike's Peak fame, had traveled up the Mississippi in 1805 from St. Louis to the mouth of what would be called the Minnesota River. Pike's mission was to determine how large the Native American populations were, what lands they inhabited, and what animal skins they traded with whom. He was instructed to appease the Indian tribes and "attach them to the United States."

At the junction of the Mississippi and Minnesota rivers, Pike camped on a small island, raising the US flag. He held a council with the Dakota tribal leaders, urging them to keep the peace with their traditional enemy the Ojibwe. He also got Dakota leaders to give up two tracts of land for American military posts. Pike marked the ceremony by handing out gifts and rum, and promising the Dakota $2,000 or its equivalent in goods.

The Dakota had lived in this area for hundreds of years, calling it *ma-ko-ce co-ka-ya-kin*—center of the earth. Sadly, more than 1,600 Dakota were forced into a camp here after the US–Dakota War of 1862. Forced to spend the winter in a cold, wet floodplain camp, hundreds of people died before they were moved out of the state.

The establishment of Fort Snelling in 1819 was an historic beginning for Minnesota, marking the start of an American presence. After the War of 1812, British fur trading companies slowly began leaving the area—either voluntarily or under pressure

Mississippi River Banks and Bluffs

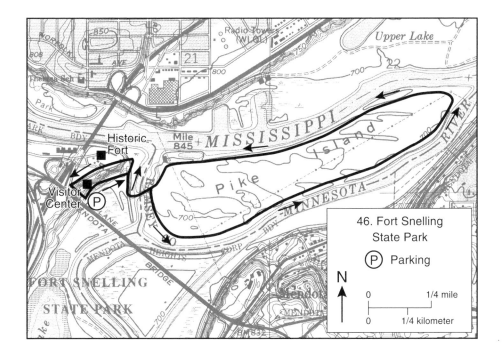

from American companies. To protect its commercial interests, the American government began building a chain of military posts stretching from Detroit to St. Louis. Major Stephen Long was sent to investigate the sites Pike had acquired and make recommendations on post sites. He chose a "high point of land, elevated about one hundred and twenty feet above the water, and fronting immediately on the Mississippi" where it met the Minnesota.

Construction began in 1820 and continued under the command of Colonel Josiah Snelling until 1827. Building the diamond-shaped, blufftop fort was hard work. Soldiers cut pine logs in the Rum River area, then floated them down to a sawmill at St. Anthony Falls. Local stone was quarried to build 10-foot-high walls.

The frontier fort was called "an isle of safety" in the wilderness, but it was more than that, according to state historian

Theodore Blegen. Frontier posts weren't "merely hubs around which vast growth and development would come with the passing decades, but also communities of civilized people whose own lives and activities were part of the unfolding culture of the Middle West." Fort Snelling became a center for dances, theater productions, and schooling.

It also played a role in one of this country's most famous legal slavery cases. Dred Scott came to Fort Snelling with his owner, the fort doctor, in 1836. Later, they moved to Missouri. After the doctor's death, Scott sued for his freedom on the grounds that living in Minnesota, an area where slavery was prohibited under the Missouri Compromise, made him a free man. The US Supreme Court denied Scott's claim, saying that because he was property, he didn't have the right to sue in the first place. A memorial to Scott lies outside the fort's walls on the river bluff.

Canopy of trees over the trail to the historic fort

Sitting in the middle of an urban area, the state park's lowland river habitat is a refuge for waterfowl. The rivers are migration corridors and good viewing areas for American coots, diving ducks, great blue herons, great egrets, pied-billed grebes, blue-winged teal, belted kingfishers, and double-crested cormorants. Along the riverbanks or in the park's lakes, snapping, soft-shelled, and wood turtles are seen.

The state park has picnic areas, a swimming beach, fishing areas, two boat ramps, canoe access to the Minnesota River, a year-round visitor center, golf course, and ball fields. There are no camping facilities. Because of the rivers, lakes, and marshes, mosquitoes can be bothersome in summer. The state park's phone number is 612-725-2389.

Operated by the Minnesota Historical Society, the recreated fort and history center are open varying days from May through October. Costumed interpreters do a good job of recreating the daily lives of soldiers, trades workers, and even the colonel and his family. Call 612-726-1171 for information or visit the historical society's web site at www.mnhs.org.

How to Get There

The park is in St. Paul, north of the intersection of I-94 and MN 5. Turn east off MN 5 onto Post Road near the Minneapolis–St.

Paul International Airport. Post Road turns north just before the park entrance.

The Trail

Drive 2 miles into the park to the visitor center lot. The trail starts on the east end of the parking lot. In about 0.1 mile, you come to a bench at a T-intersection by the Minnesota River. You are nearly under the Mendota Bridge, and unfortunately you will hear traffic and airplane noise on this hike.

Turn left and follow the trail through a floodplain forest of tall cottonwoods. Blooming white snakeroot and white and purple aster were prolific when we hiked in September. The trail curves left. Cross a bridge over a small channel between the two rivers. Across the bridge are signs with information about Pike's Island and the river islands.

Turn right, following the Hiking Club sign. The trail moves toward the Minnesota River and continues to hug the sandy bank. Pass a trail on your left, with a bench, that cuts to the other side of the island loop. Continue through the area of thick maples and shrubby underbrush. Pass another trail that crosses to the other side of the island.

The Mississippi and Minnesota rivers meet about 1.9 miles from the start of this hike. Walk down to the point of the island to look at the line of sediment that forms where the rivers meet. There's also a bench if you want to take in the view for awhile.

From the confluence, turn left and continue along the sandy shore of the Mississippi. Pass by the cut-over trail, now on your left. The trees are more open along this section, and you soon come to an area of very large cottonwoods. Short trails lead down to the riverbank, where motorboaters may be anchored. You also pass a marina. Huge cottonwood trees grow here.

The second cut-over trail comes in to your left. Continue straight ahead, then bear left to the Pike Island interpretive signs. Cross the bridge again, and turn right. Shortly you meet the paved Historic Fort Snelling Trail. A spur trail to the right leads to the old Fort Snelling boat landing, and just past that is a trail to Minnehaha Falls, marked with a sign.

The trail curves to your left and angles up the bluff, following the path of the old boat landing road, the oldest in Minnesota. The remains of large stone blocks that supported a later roadway can be seen in the trees to your right.

The trail comes to the top of the bluff beneath the South Battery. Stairs to your right lead to the re-created fort. If the fort is open, it's worth a visit.

If you decide not to, continue straight ahead. You're now walking along the top of the bluff. Pass a path, to your right, that leads to the fort's gate.

The trail passes where the fort's gardens used to be and into an area of trees. At a stone with a commemorative plaque, turn left and descend the steps behind the visitor center. Because this area was used as the fort's dump, nonnative plants like catnip, Siberian elm, garlic mustard, and buckthorn have taken hold here. Walk around the visitor's center to the parking area. A memorial to the 1862 Dakota prisoners is located just north of the parking lot. The somber monument's center is made of pipestone.

47

Frontenac State Park

Total distance: 3 miles

Approximate hiking time: 2 hours

Difficulty: Moderate with difficult spots

Vertical rise: 300 feet

Maps: USGS 7½' Maiden Rock quad, Minnesota Department of Natural Resources state park map

Humans have inhabited the bluffs along Lake Pepin, a wide spot in the Mississippi River, since about 400 BC. State archaeologists have excavated remains of the Hopewell Indian culture here. Unlike many native cultures in mid-America and the plains, the stationary Hopewellians lived along major waterways and tended crops of squash, sunflowers, little barley, and some maize. They established trade routes across the country and used native copper and silver to make metal tools. Frontenac State Park is about as far north as the Hopewell culture lived.

Next came Dakota and Fox tribes, hunting and fishing along the riverbank. These tribes considered an area at the north end of the park, and its large rock with an opening, sacred.

Europeans came through beginning in 1680. In 1727, a party of French explorers built a log stockade in the park's vicinity, then abandoned the post when the British claimed much of North America after the French and Indian War, or Seven Years' War. Fur trader James "Bully" Wells was the first permanent settler and built a trading post and home south of the park, where the town of Frontenac now is located. The fur trade ended, and logging became the dominant industry. Most of the old-growth forest around the park was cut down, and huge rafts of logs floated down the Mississippi to sawmills.

After coming to the area to hunt, Israel Garrard decided to stay. He platted a 320-acre town, which he named Frontenac in

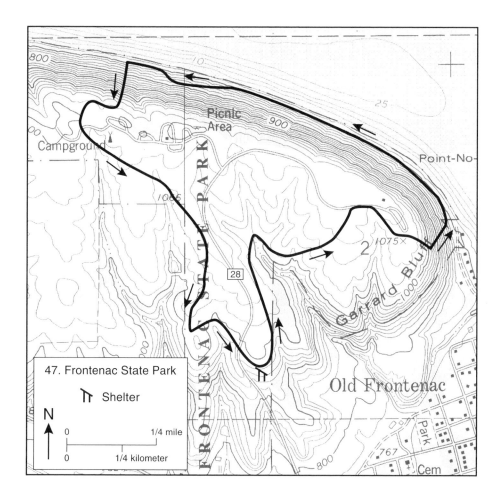

47. Frontenac State Park

🛖 Shelter

N

0 — 1/4 mile
0 — 1/4 kilometer

honor of a French colonial governor who sponsored early exploratory expeditions. The town grew, and by the 1870s it was a fashionable summer resort area. Steamboats brought wealthy people to stay at the Lake Side Hotel, with its three stories and double porches. When railroads eclipsed river travel, many Mississippi River towns faded away. Some of old Frontenac's buildings can be visited, and the original Christ Episcopal Church still holds Sunday services.

The National Park Service took note of the area in 1935, but it wasn't until 1954 that a group started working successfully to preserve the area's natural beauty and historical significance. Local people raised money to buy an important tract of land, and the state legislature established Frontenac State Park in 1957.

The landscape that local residents wanted to preserve is a 3-mile-long bluff that rises 450 feet above Lake Pepin. Millions of years ago, a vast sea covered what is now Minnesota. Sediment piled up on the bottom and slowly turned to rock. Huge Glacial River Warren then began carving across the state as it headed for what is now the eastern border. Joined by meltwaters from the

In Yan Teopa rock formation

upper St. Croix and Mississippi Rivers, the powerful ancient waterway carved through the limestone of Frontenac State Park. At the turn of the 20th century, limestone was a popular building material. A quarry operated in the park area, located below the picnic area. Architects chose this rock to build the Cathedral of St. John the Divine in New York in 1883.

Lake Pepin exists because downriver, the faster-flowing Chippewa River carried heavier sediment when it joined the Mississippi. When this sediment settled, it created a natural dam that caused the Mississippi to swell onto a wider flood plain. At the north end of the park, Lake Pepin is nearly 2.5 miles wide. Many boaters and sailors use this wide spot, which extends upstream for 25 miles.

The 2,230-acre park has a semimodern campground with 58 sites, 19 with electricity. A trailer dump station with showers and flush toilets is available. Four rustic walk-in campsites are located centrally among the hiking trails. A primitive group camp has running water, and a picnic ground is equipped with electricity. The park's telephone number is 651-345-3401.

How to Get There

Located 10 miles southeast of Red Wing, the park is off MN 61, part of the Great River Road. Turn northeast onto Goodhue County 2 and drive about 1 mile to the park entrance. Turn left to the information office and park headquarters. Continue to the park's picnic area.

The Trail

Park in the picnic area lot. The trails at this park can be confusing, but it's easy to keep the river in sight and head toward it. The trails that parallel the river are on a bluff that descends nearly 45 degrees. In several spots, the angle induces mild vertigo, so exercise caution.

Near the information kiosk, head toward the river on a gravel path. Descend steps to an overlook of the river to your right. Stay to the left on a trail with interpretive signs, which continues down the steep bluff. Cross a wooden bridge, then more steps as the trail descends in switchbacks. At a mapboard with a bench, turn left toward the river and descend more steps. A trail intersection is marked with a sign reading CAMPGROUND. Go straight ahead on this path. Cross a wooden bridge over a hole left by an uprooted tree. A lot of trees are down here. A June 1998 windstorm took its toll on shallow-rooted maples.

At an intersection, a trail to the right leads down steps to the riverbank. To the left is the Half-Way Trail, which leads to the top of the bluff. Continue straight ahead. For the next 0.6 mile you walk parallel to the river. Maple and oak have grown up to replace the old forest and grow thickly along the steep bluff. When we hiked in September, leaves had started to fall, opening up the canopy to let brilliant golden light fall on the trail.

Now the trail turns left and heads up the bluff, toward the campground, on a narrow path with switchbacks and more than 100 wood and stone steps. You come to a large rock with an opening, called *In Yan Teopa* in Dakota. The relatively soft limestone has been worn away into this unusual shape with a hole in the middle.

Just up from *In Yan Teopa,* a trail to the left heads back to the picnic area. Go right up the steps to the campground. Cross the park road and follow the trail as it curves back toward the picnic area. The mowed grass trail here goes through slightly rolling prairie with pockets of shrubs. Cross-country ski trails intersect the trails used on this hike. If you find

A view of Lake Pepin

yourself off the described route, turn east, and keep heading toward the river.

In about 0.8 mile, turn left on a trail that shortly crosses the park road, then curves to the right. You come to a park shelter with a wide, open view of the prairie and river beyond.

From the shelter, the trail turns to the left. Pass by a trail to your left, and shortly you meet an intersection with the Hiking Club trail. Turn left and walk past large oak and cottonwood trees. The trail ascends for nearly 0.2 mile to a spur trail to the Eagle Point overlook. Turn right and walk about 0.2 mile to the overlook.

Head back to the main trail. Stay on the Hiking Club route as you pass several other trails. You should cross a bridge over a small stream in a valley, with a deep ravine to your right. This is where the walk-in campsites are located, so the trails can be confusing. Stay on the Hiking Club trail, to your right.

At a four-way intersection, go straight ahead on the Hiking Club trail. Meet the park road at the overflow parking area, turn right, and walk along it to the picnic area.

48

Great River Bluffs State Park

Total distance: 5.7 miles

*Approximate hiking time: 3 hours,
15 minutes*

Difficulty: Easy to moderate

Vertical rise: 50 feet

*Maps: USGS 7½' Pickwick quad,
Minnesota Department of Natural
Resources state park map*

Great River Bluffs is in Minnesota's geologic driftless area, a small region that missed out on the last series of glaciers. It lacks the glacial drift—dirt, gravel, rocks, and boulders—that covers the rest of the state. That doesn't mean that earlier glaciers didn't affect the landscape here. The half-dome bluffs, sheer rock cliffs, steep valley walls, rolling uplands, and flat floodplain were shaped in part by these vast ice sheets. Glacial runoff rushed down streams into the Mississippi River, increasing its eroding power. The waters carved hundreds of feet through the sedimentary rock of the area—limestone, sandstone, and shale.

So, where did the soil in this part of Minnesota come from? Fine clay dust, called loess, from glacial outwash and alluvial plains blew into southeastern Minnesota. The soil holds moisture and works for farming, but it's also easily eroded.

Native Americans who lived and traveled along these bluffs for centuries built burial mounds and other mounds whose purpose is unknown. Sadly, none of the mounds known to have been within or next to the park remain. Highway and housing construction destroyed them.

The bluffs affect the microclimates found at Great River Bluffs State Park. Slopes of up to 50 degrees occur on the south-southwest side of the bluffs. Even in winter, the slopes can take in a lot of heat from the sun. Of course, at night they cool off greatly. This constant freezing and thawing makes it impossible for woody plants to take hold, while grasses and flowering

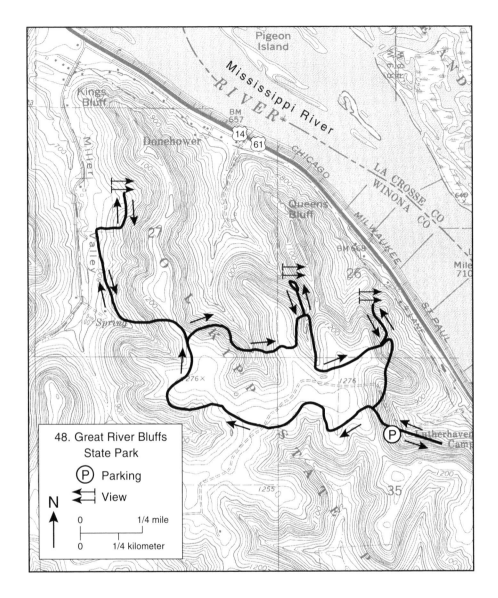

48. Great River Bluffs
State Park

P Parking

N View

0   1/4 mile
0   1/4 kilometer

plants do well. This unique and fragile habitat is called a goat prairie, for the nimble mountain-climbing animals.

On the north and east sides of the slopes, hardwood trees and shrubs grow in the more even temperatures. The first settlers in the area plowed the upland and floodplain for crops, eliminating trees and causing erosion. The objective of the park's management plan is to return native trees like white pine, basswood, maple, green ash, and oak and to restore native prairie.

Wildlife found in the park include opossums, spotted skunks, black squirrels, coyotes, vultures, and wild turkeys. Eagles can be seen floating above the Mississippi River.

The Mississippi River

The endangered timber rattlesnake lives in the park, but sightings are rare.

The park is within the Richard J. Dorer Memorial Hardwood State Forest, established in 1961 to control erosion and manage the forest. People in the area also were asking for more recreational activities, and some state forest lands were transferred to form the state park in 1976. It is one of Minnesota's "natural state parks" that emphasize "protection, perpetuation, and restoration of natural resources." In these state parks (Crosby-Manitou is another example) only facilities needed "to complement the resources and values being preserved" are developed.

The park has a campground with 31 sites (no electricity), a group camp with pit toilets and water, a five-site bicycle camp with vault toilets and water, and picnic grounds with tables, grills, water, and toilets. To contact the park, call 507-643-6849.

How to Get There

From Winona, drive southeast about 20 miles to the intersection of MN 61 and I-90, at the small town of Dakota. Head west on I-90 for about 4 miles. Turn north at exit 266 onto Winona County 12, then almost immediately turn northeast onto CR 3, which part of the Apple Blossom Scenic Drive. Continue on CR 3 for about 1.1 miles to the park entrance on the east side of the road.

The Trail

Drive to the park's campground, passing the King's Bluff Trail parking area and the road to the picnic grounds, both on your left. Park in the campground's visitor area, also to your left.

Find the trail at the north end of the parking area and turn right to the first of several scenic overlooks on this hike. You're about 600 feet above the Mississippi, but the trails follow the blufftops with relatively little change in elevation. The shredded bark trail here follows the top of a ridge for about 0.2 mile. The view is of the Mississippi River to the southeast.

Head back to the trail intersection, with a mapboard that still shows the park's previous name of O. L. Kipp State Park, and bear right. For the next 0.3 mile, the trail parallels the park road, then crosses it at the entrance to the group camp on your left. Turn left at another mapboard sign. It had rained the night before we last hiked here, and the packed earth trail was very slippery. A descent takes you to an intersection with a spur trail that leads left 0.3 mile to the group camp and scenic views of the bluffs and valley west of the park.

Back on the main trail, head left, and the trail ascends. At a T-intersection, turn left onto a trail marked with a sign indicating the trail is moderately difficult. For the next 0.5 mile, the trail does take moderate ups and downs through maple, ash, and oak. Pale lavender wild geraniums were blooming during a Memorial Day weekend hike.

Cross-country ski trails intersect in this section of the park, and they aren't indicated on the summer trails map. This can be confusing. Bear left again at an intersection with a map and "moderate difficulty" sign. At the next trail sign, continue straight ahead, passing a trail to your right that leads to the picnic area.

Now you cross the park road at the King's Bluff Trail parking area. Continue straight ahead onto this trail, which also is marked with a Hiking Club sign. This is where you'll see information and warnings about timber rattlesnakes. After about 0.1 mile is another trail to the picnic area. Continue straight ahead. Another interpretive sign tells you that this is one of the few areas where the Henslow's sparrow nests.

The wide mowed path continues to a Y-intersection. Turn left onto an interpretive nature trail, which curves around an area of ash and white pine for about 0.4 mile before meeting back up with the King's Bluff Trail. This four-way intersection provides a view of a valley between King's and Queen's Bluff to the northeast and the Mississippi River to the southeast. King's and Queen's Bluffs are state Scientific and Natural Areas. However, Queen's Bluff, a prime example of goat prairie, is accessible only if you have a permit.

About 1.2 miles from the King's Bluff Trail parking area, you reach the end point. A sign provides information about the geology of the bluff. When you're ready, head back the way you came. At the overlook intersection, turn left to the picnic area. Cross-country ski trails intersect this section, so check the maps to make sure you're still headed toward the picnic area. A spur trail to another overlook intersects to your left. Take it if you wish; it's a closer view of Queen's Bluff.

Back on this hike's route, continue past the overlook intersection for a little over 0.1 mile to a four-way intersection. Turn left toward the picnic area, where water is available if you need it. Pick up the trail at the northeast end of the parking area. The trail curves to the east, then intersects with two overlook spurs. After checking out either or both of the overlooks, turn left. After about 0.3 mile, cross the park road. In a few paces, you come to the T-intersection you passed on the first part of the hike. Turn left. It was dusk, and we saw about five white-tailed deer in this forested area. Continue to the intersection that leads to the group camp, this time to your right. Two black squirrels ran up a tree as we passed. Cross the park road again, and you're heading back to the campground parking area.

49

Richard J. Dorer Memorial Hardwood State Forest, Trout Valley Unit

Total distance: 7 miles

Approximate hiking time: 3.5 hours

Difficulty: Steep climbs up bluffs

Vertical rise: 440 feet

Maps: USGS 7½' Weaver quad, Minnesota Department of Natural Resources state park map

Despite its high bluffs and valleys, southeastern Minnesota was one of the first areas to be cleared for farming. Settlers plowed and planted crops or created pastures on steep bluff slopes. After decades of such farming, erosion had carved gullies into the clay soil, which washed down into rivers and streams. Floods and mudslides were common. Burning and improper cutting caused defective and deformed second-growth trees.

Richard J. Dorer was supervisor of wildlife development for the Minnesota Department of Conservation in the 1940s and 1950s. He developed and promoted a plan to improve woodland management and recover land previously used for farming. It took until 1960 to get the seven proposed counties on board. County commissioners donated land, and the state bought erosion-prone property around these parcels.

The Memorial Hardwood State Forest was officially established in March 1960. Bluff slopes were replanted with trees and shrubs, and runoff ponds were built to halt erosion. Wildlife management areas and state parks were created. It was renamed to honor Dorer after he died in 1974.

The forest is divided into several management units. The Trout Valley Unit is 2,375 acres of steep, wooded ridges and bluffs that run along spring-fed Trout Valley Creek. Oak, hickory, aspen, birch, and black walnut were planted along the steep bluffsides. The valleys are a mix of pasture, woods, and farmland. Interestingly, local farmers plant crops on the flat blufftops.

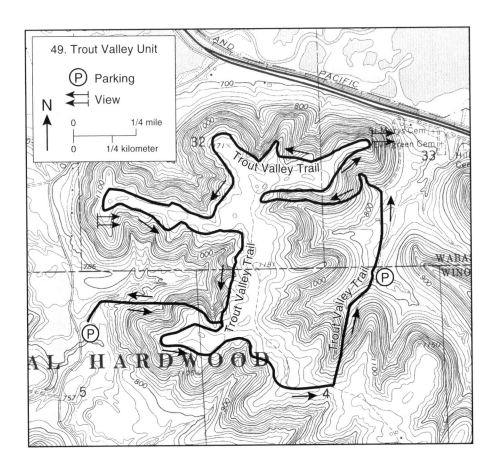

49. Trout Valley Unit

Ⓟ Parking

↞ View

N

0 — 1/4 mile

0 — 1/4 kilometer

Several of the other Dorer forest units have developed campgrounds, but the trail is Trout Valley's primary recreational feature. It is open to horses, mountain bikes, motorcycles, all-terrain vehicles, and snowmobiles in the winter.

How to Get There

From Wabasha, drive south on MN 61 to the small town of Weaver. Continue south on MN 61 for 2 miles to Wabasha County 29 and turn west. In about 1.3 miles, you cross the county line and the road becomes Winona County 31. It is 0.1 mile to the unit's entrance on the east side of the road, to your left.

The Trail

Park anywhere along the flat, open grassy area. There is a pit toilet here. Because of ATV use, the immediate area around the trail's beginning looks rough in spots. But despite two groups of campers at the trail head, we met only one man putting along on a four-wheeler during the 7-mile hike.

The trail starts to the east and is marked with a sign. You immediately begin a 300-foot ascent to the top of the bluff. The trail is a wide gravel path with erosion barriers set across it. Pass a trail to your left that loops back to the trailhead. Continue up the steep slope to a wide intersection that ATVs use to turn around.

Bluffs west of the Mississippi River

Turn right. A sign marks the Trout Valley Trail. Now the trail is level as you pass through an open area of shrubs and wildflowers. During an August hike, wild bergamot, goldenrod, Queen Anne's lace, yarrow, fleabane, asters, yellow coneflowers, evening primrose, and white campion were blooming. The large variety of wildflowers attracts a number of butterflies.

Pass a tree plantation to your left. Continue on the trail, which resembles a very narrow country road. Lots of deer tracks could be seen on the trail. In one spot, pine trees form a tunnel. The trail makes several gentle ascents and descents, curving right and left until you come to the field of corn on your left. After coming up through the trees, then the grass and wildflowers, the cultivated farmland is a surprise.

The trail skirts the edge of the field for about 0.5 mile, then heads toward the woods. Come to an intersection with a rough road closed off farther down by a red metal gate. To your left is a Trout Valley Trail sign where the path descends through a heavily wooded area. The trail is wide but rocky as it makes a steep descent into the valley between two bluffs.

At the bottom of the valley is a parking area where a snowmobile trail, which was closed by a gate, heads southeast. Follow the narrow road to your left to a gate with an orange triangular Trout Valley Trail sign. The next 0.6 mile is a steep ascent up the bluff. A patch of orange blackberry lily grows along the trail.

The trail makes a hairpin turn to the right and continues through a more open area along the blufftop. Young red pines are mixed in with the shrubs here. Soon the Mississippi River comes into view as the trail curves left. Turn right at the VISTA sign. An overlook, high above MN 61, lets you look far up and down the river and over to Wisconsin. As if on cue, a bald eagle flew just above our heads.

Return to the main trail and turn right. It's about 1.5 miles from the Mississippi River vista to the next overlook on the west side of the unit as the trail follows narrow arms of the bluff. The trail makes slight ups and downs and passes a farm field to your left. Pass by a trail to your left that cuts across the blufftop.

Soon you pass the other end of the cornfield, also on your left. Enter a wooded area of pine and birch. The dirt trail is so hard packed here it feels like pavement. You pass an area of tall pines along this section, which mostly stays in the woods. Pass by an intersection with a snowmobile trail to your right.

The trail makes a 90-degree turn left. The next overlook has a railing facing west above the bluffs and valleys. Another 90-degree left turn takes the trail parallel to the way you came, a bit farther south in the woods. The gentle ups and downs continue, and there are several breaks in the trees where you can again look out on the bluff valleys. When you return to the cornfield, the trail turns right and continues along its edge. A marshy area on the left comes just before the wide intersection with the trail back to the parking area. Watch your step on the steep descent.

Mississippi River Banks and Bluffs

50

Spring Lake Park Reserve

Total distance: 3 miles

Approximate hiking time: 1 hour, 45 minutes

Difficulty: Easy

Vertical rise: 50 feet

Maps: USGS 7½' St. Paul Park quad, Dakota County parks map

Over thousands of years, the Mississippi River's volume changed many times. It filled with sediment, then cut through it—a cycle that left layers of rocky terraces. As the last glacier to cover Minnesota melted into enormous Lake Agassiz, it was drained through Glacial River Warren flowing west to east. This water entered the Mississippi River valley near present-day Fort Snelling, cutting a deep trench in the glacial gravel and bedrock. As the flow of Glacial River Warren subsided, tributaries in the wide, deep valley continued to bring in sediment. Natural dams built up and created a series of channels, backwaters, deltas, dunes, lakes, and islands. The river itself flows through a small portion of the old river valley. At Spring Lake Park, the Mississippi is about 1 mile across, making this one of its widest points in the state.

The park's namesake Spring Lake, named because it was spring fed, was separated from the river by a narrow strip of land. It disappeared when Lock and Dam No. 2 was built to the south at Hastings. The lock and dam flooded most of the strip, leaving only long, narrow islands. The springs that fed the lake still are here, making this area of the Mississippi cooler and clearer than in other spots.

Spring Lake Park Reserve is a Dakota County park made up of several units. Hiking trails and picnic areas are located at the Schaar's Bluff unit.

Across from the reserve is Grey Cloud Island. Native Americans lived here 3,000

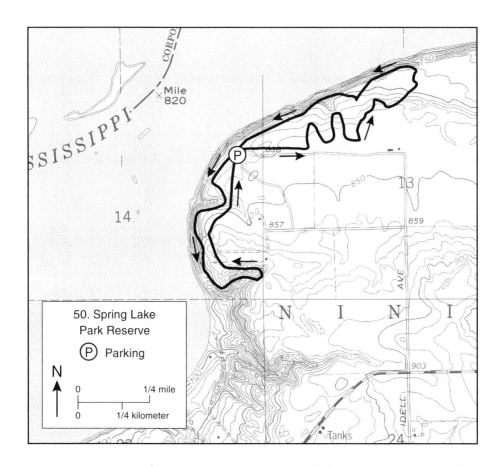

50. Spring Lake
Park Reserve

Ⓟ Parking

N

0 _____ 1/4 mile
0 _____ 1/4 kilometer

years ago, and the name apparently comes from Chief Grey Cloud and a woman who was an influential member of the Wabasha family named Grey Cloud Woman. Also across the river, two sandy terraces called Grey Cloud Dunes rise 40 to 110 feet above the river. This unique habitat is a state Scientific and Natural Area and contains rare sea-beach needlegrass. Purple sand grass, Illinois tick trefoil, long-bearded hawk-weed, Louisiana broomrape, and Hill's this-tle also can be found. Hiking is allowed at Grey Cloud Dunes, but there are no marked trails or maps. Visitors are encouraged to tread lightly in this unique, protected habitat.

How to Get There

From Minneapolis–St. Paul, drive east on I-494 to MN 55 and head south. MN 55 heads east as MN 52 continues south to Rochester. Continue on MN 55 about 4.5 miles to East Dakota County 42 and turn northeast, to your left. In about 1.8 miles is a large Spring Lake Park Reserve sign on Idell Avenue. Head north, a left-hand turn, 1 mile to the metal Schaar's Bluff arch.

The Trail

Park near the picnic area, where there is a small building with flush toilets. Walk on the asphalt pathway to the right of the toilets.

Bluff along the Mississippi River

Islands in the Mississippi River

The trail starts to your left just before the playground and is marked with a green hiking sign and a blue cross-country skiing sign. The wide, packed dirt trail enters a dense area of young maple and ash trees with some very tall oaks. Lots of white snakeroot grows on the forest floor here.

At a T-intersection, turn left. The trail winds its way through the mixed hardwood forest and makes a few very gentle ascents and descents. At a wide four-way intersection with a bench and a map, turn right. At the next intersection, in about 0.2 mile, stay to your right again.

At a sign reading DANGER CLIFF AHEAD, NO FENCE, the trail makes a sharp left. The path narrows, and you pass small rock ledges that give a hint of the higher bluff to come. You can see the Mississippi River through the trees to your right. This section has lots of moss-covered rocks and some roots in the trail. Some birch grow among the mostly maple forest.

Spur trails lead to overlooks along the bluff edge, but be careful. There are no railings, and the moss-covered rocks are slippery. Pass several large random boulders. Solomon's seal and white asters grow along the path.

Next comes a dense section of maple, and the rocky trail twists down steeply in a switchback to a split stone bridge over the ravine bottom. A stone path leads along the ravine to a small stone terrace. The stonework gave the lush area the look of a fairy glen.

A path to your right leads down the steep, rocky ravine to the river. To your left are 55 well-made wooden steps to the blufftop, where there is a bench.

At the next intersection, with a map, stay to your right. Here, violets and yellow avens, which were past their bloom time, grew on the forest floor. Soon you come to the start of a wooden rail fence that runs along the bluff top through the picnic area. Walk along the fence and turn left where the mowed area meets taller grass. Head back up to the asphalt path and turn right. Several interpretive signs provide information about the river.

Continue straight ahead as the asphalt ends, and the trail narrows and moves toward the river bluff. Here weathered cedar grows precariously along the stone bluff. The trees open up a bit, and you come to an intersection with a map and bench. Go straight ahead along the river. The trail goes down and up a moderately steep wooded ravine, then continues gentle ascents and descents through an area with more oak.

In an open area, the trail takes a sharp left away from the river and heads through a tunnel of sumac. The wide mowed path passes through a small area of pine trees.

Shortly, you come to a T-intersection where you turn left. Stay to your left as you pass a trail to the right, and you should see a farm silo straight ahead. The trail heads through another small area of pine, where orange fallen needles cushioned the path.

Enter an open area with woods to your left and a grassy field to your right. Shortly you can see the tops of buildings in the maintenance area through the trees. The next intersection is a convergence of three mowed paths. Either of the trails to your right leads you back to the wide grassy area adjacent to the parking lot. As we left the park, we pulled up next to a hawk sitting atop a large wooden signpost, surveying the field across the road. It was still sitting there as we drove away.

Resources

History of the Santee Sioux, United States Indian Policy on Trial by Roy W. Meyer. Lincoln, NE: University of Nebraska Press, 1967 and 1993.

Minnesota: A History of the State by Theodore C. Blegen. Minneapolis: University of Minnesota Press, 1963 and 1975.

Minnesota Underfoot: A Field Guide to the State's Outstanding Geologic Features by Constance J. Sansome. Stillwater, MN: Voyageur Press, 1983.

Minnesota's Geographic Names by Warren Upham. St. Paul: Minnesota Historical Society, 1920 and 1969.

Minnesota's Geology by Richard Ojakangas and Charles L. Matsch. Minneapolis: University of Minnesota Press, 1982.

Index

French and Indian War, 18, 208
French explorers, 18
Frogs, 197
Frontenac, 208, 209
Frontenac State Park, 208–212
Fur trade, 18, 53, 58, 76, 92, 99, 122, 125, 204, 208

G

Garlic mustard, 207
Garrard, Israel, 208, 209
Gaultier, Pierre, 18, 125
Geese, 185, 191
Gentian, 179
Geology, 15–16
George H. Crosby–Manitou State Park, 43–46
George Washington Memorial Pines Trail, 103–105
Gettysburg, 66, 67
Ginger, wild, 153, 161
Gitchi Gami State Trail, 87
Glacial debris drift, 17, 151, 196
Glacial Lake Agassiz, 18, 147, 148, 184, 196, 221
Glacial Lakes State Park, 177–179
Glacial River Warren, 16, 147, 148, 184, 196, 209, 221
Glaciers, 15–17, 28, 31, 39, 41, 62, 66, 70, 80, 92, 96, 99, 100, 102, 106, 115, 126, 139, 143, 154, 165, 169, 177, 180
Glenwood, 178
Gneiss, 15
Goat prairie, 214, 216
Goldenrod, 41, 42, 74, 101, 137, 150, 155, 166, 178, 191, 194, 198, 219
Goodhue County, 211
Gooseberry Falls State Park, 37, 47–49, 81, 83
Gooseberry River, 47
Grackles, 183
Grand Bois, 151
Grand Marais, 23, 103, 105, 106
Grand Marais Boy Scout Troop No. 67, 103
Grand Portage, 19, 125, 126
Grand Portage National Monument, 21
Grand Portage of the St. Louis, 58
Grand Portage State Park, 50–53, 120
Granite, 15, 66, 113, 126
Granite Falls, 197
Grant, Ulysses S., II, 106
Grasses, 16, 18
Gray-headed coneflower, 155, 181, 198
Gray wolves, 110
Graywacke, 60, 61
Great blue herons, 206

Great Britain, 18, 204
Great egrets, 206
Great horned owls, 111
Great River Bluffs State Park, 213–216
Grebes, 143, 206
Greenstone, 30, 31, 126
Grey Cloud, Chief, 222
Grey Cloud Dunes, 222
Grey Cloud Island, 221
Grey Cloud Woman, 222
Greysolon, Daniel, 69
Groseilliers, Sieur Médard des, 18, 47
Groundwater, 18
Grouse, 65, 111, 143
The Guide to the Superior Hiking Trail, 22
Gumweed, 166
Gunflint Trail, 22, 23, 103, 105

H

Hackberry, 176
Hair-like beak rush, 18
Half-dome bluffs, 213
Half-Way Trail, 211
Harebell, 52, 56
Hastings, 221
Hawks, 65, 132, 143, 225
Hawkweed, 52, 98, 222
Hawthorns, 181
Heart-leaved Alexander, 18
Hegman Lake, 99
Hell's Gate Rapids, 29
Hell's Gate Trail, 29
Hematite, 33
Henslow's sparrows, 216
Hepaticas, 41, 153
Herons, 181, 206
Hibbing, 96
Hickory Bridge, 152
Hidden Falls, 37, 117, 152, 153
High Falls: Baptism River, 119–121; Pigeon River, 51
High Falls Trail, 52, 120
High Landing campsite, 61
Hikes: difficulty of, 6–11, 24; features of, 6–11; Minnesota map of, 12
Hiking: gear for, 23; guidelines for, 24; long-distance, 21–23
Hiking Club Trail, 29; Afton State Park, 132–133; Cascade River State Park, 37; Crow Wing State Park, 202; Fort Ridgely State Park, 176; Fort Snelling State Park, 207; Frontenac State Park, 212; George H. Crosby–Manitou State Park, 45; Glacial Lakes State Park, 179; Great River Bluffs

L

Labrador tea, 113
Lac qui Parle River, 186
Lac qui Parle State Park, 184–187
Lac qui Parle Wildlife Management Area, 185
Lady's slipper, 61, 170
Lake Agassiz, 16
Lake Andrew, 156–157
Lake Andrew Trail, 156
Lake Athabasca, 122
Lake Bensen, 46
Lake County, 99
Lake Duluth, 16
Lake Itasca, 54
Lake Maria State Park, 143–146
Lake of the Woods, 18
Lake Pepin, 208, 209, 211, 212
Lake Shumway, 78, 79
Lake Shumway Trail, 78
Lake Side Hotel, 209
Lake Superior, 16, 18, 20, 27, 46, 52, 117, 120, 121
Lake Vermilion, 30
Lake Walk, Superior Hiking Trail, 66–68
Lakeview Trail, 157
Land cession treaty, 195
Larch, 89
Lava, 35, 43, 47, 48, 51, 62, 68, 72, 84, 110, 114, 118, 139
Leadplant, 156, 178, 194
Leaf Hills, 177
Lemmings, 78
Leveaux Mountain, 74
Lichens, 16, 52, 113, 117, 167
Lighthouse, Split Rock, 83, 84, 86
Limestone, 15, 151, 159, 211, 213
Lincoln, Abraham, 174, 188
Little barley, 208
Little bluestem, 17, 177, 181
Little Crow, Chief, 173, 174, 188, 195
Little Mount Tom, 156
Little Prairie Loop, 149
Little Two Harbors, 85
Little Two Harbors Trail, 87
Lock and Dam No. 2, 221
Lodge-to-lodge hiking, 22
Lodges, 22
Loess, 213
Log cabins, 118
Log lodges, 128
Logging, 16, 19, 30, 47, 70, 72–73, 80–81, 85, 89, 96, 99, 100, 118, 122, 128, 141, 142, 151, 208
Long, Stephen, 205

Long-bearded hawkweed, 222
Long-distance hiking, 21–23
Loon Lake, 78
Loons, 56, 143
Lost Lake Trail, 113
Louisiana broomrape, 222
Louisiana Purchase, 19
Louisville Swamp Unit, 129, 147–150
Low Lake, 100, 102
Lowell, Michigan, 23
Lower Cliffline Trail, 167
Lower Falls of Gooseberry River, 48, 49
Lower Mound Lake, 167
Lower Sioux Agency, 195
Lower Sioux Agency Historic Site, 173, 188–190
Lower Sioux Community, 189
Lower Valley Trail, 175–176
Luht, Sieur du, 69
Luverne, 166
Lynx, 110

M

Ma-ko-ce co-ka-ya-kin (term), 204
Madeline Island, 66
Magma, 106
Magnetite, 33
Magney, Clarence R., 63
Maiden Rock, Wisconsin, 158
Maidenhair ferns, 94
Maize, 208
Manfred, Frederick, 166
Manitou, 43
Manitou River, 43, 45
Mankato, 174, 189
Maple, 17
Maple Ridge Trail, 137
Maps, 23; Afton State Park, 130; Banning State Park, 26; Bass Lake Trail, 100; Bear Head Lake State Park, 31; Blue Mounds State Park, 164; Buffalo River State Park, 170; Cascade River State Park, 34; Chippewa National Forest Shingobee, 41; Crow Wing State Park, 200; Eagle Mountain Trail, 107; Forestville/Mystery Cave State Park, 134; Fort Ridgely State Park, 174; Fort Snelling State Park, 205; Frontenac State Park, 209; George H. Crosby–Manitou State Park, 44; George Washington Memorial Pines Trail, 105; Glacial Lakes State Park, 178; Gooseberry Falls State Park, 48; Grand Portage State Park, 51; Great River Bluffs State Park, 214; Interstate State Park, 141; Itasca State Park, 55; Jay Cooke State Park,

T

Index

Wild onion, 166
Wild rice, 69, 125
Wild rose, 41, 65, 98
Wild turkeys, 135, 214
Wilder, Laura Ingalls, 151
Wilderness Act (1964), 110
Wilderness Drive, 56
Wildfires, 21
Wildlife refuges, 147–150
Willmar, 155, 177
Winchell, Newton, 106
Windom, 182, 183
Winona, 158, 161, 215
Winona County, 215, 218
Wisconsin Age glacier, 143
Wissakode zibi (term), 62
Wolf Lake, 79
Wolves, 65, 110
Wood anemone, 65
Wood ducks, 181
Wood Lake, 173
Wood lily, 18
Wood nettle, 153
Wood turtles, 206
Woodpeckers, 65, 111
Works Progress Administration, 92, 191

Y

Yankton Dakota people, 168
Yarrow, 52, 191, 219
Yellow Banks, 92
Yellow birch, 43
Yellow Birch Trail, 46
Yellow coneflowers, 219
Yellow hawkweed, 52
Yellow jewelweed, 178
Yellow lady's slipper, 61
Yellow Medicine, 190
Yellow Medicine Agency, 195
Yellow Medicine River, 195, 197, 198
Yellow medicine (roots), 195
Yellow pond lily, 107
Yellow sarsaparilla, 195
Yellow warblers, 170
Youth Conservation Corps, 74, 103

Z

Zeolite, 48